Bless
me
Father

Ge'ko Publishing | www.gekopublishing.co.za

First Published by Ge'ko Publishing
10 Louis Road, Orchards, Johannesburg, South Africa

ISBN 978-0-9802556-4-5

Cover artwork by Nelson Makamo

Designed at BKOdesign+garage (Jhb)
www.bko.co.za/designgarage
Book design by Phehello Mofokeng

Ge'ko
publishing

Bless Me Father

by Mario d'Offizi

For my wife Carla, and my children Paul,
Gianni, Gabriella and Mirella; and my good
friend, the late Gerrie Wagenaar, all of
whose belief in me was much stronger than
mine.

Acknow ledge ments

Without my publisher and editor, Andrew Miller, this book would not have been written. Not now, and not in the way it has been. It was Andrew's faith in me, his encouragement, advice, guidance, superb editing (with some critical suggestions and rewrites in places), and the final arrangement of the book into some sense of sequence, order and chronology, that made it all possible.

The technical editing, input and suggestions of Maureen Miller, who left no stone unturned in her quest to make this book as error-free and readable as possible, have also been invaluable. A special thank-you too, to my young friend LONi, who stirred the beginnings of this book. After reading some of my short stories and poems – and the initial, tentative pages of this book – months before I visited the DRC, he suggested that I keep going. When I admitted that I did not know where to begin to write my story, he offered to help and spent countless hours interviewing me and helping me to think back on the past.

8

We live in a world of absolutes. It is tempting to blame modern media for our collective tendency to see the world as one of issues and solutions, but this is a little naïve. Look back as far as you want in history and you will see people treating highly complex aspects of life in simplistic terms. Perhaps it is this ability that allows us to survive our challenges and move forward.

When it comes to issues such as child abuse, however, there is no doubt that we are significantly impacted by our media environment. Such is the media prominence given to this age-old problem that we – ordinary citizens – are reflex in our reactions to it. We expect, and generally we experience, a defined range of near-generic explanations of the impact of abuse on the child, and later, the adult.

I believe that life is more complicated than our stock phrases are able to appreciate, or articulate.

Mario d'Offizi has lived his life in this complicated grey area of event, reaction and delayed response. *Bless Me Father* tells his story and describes his experiences while moving through this troubled and troubling land. For me, the most remarkable thing about *Bless Me Father* is the softness with which the author treats his own life and experiences, many of which are deeply shocking to the reader.

Abuse (sexual and otherwise) runs through Mario d'Offizi's life, and hence through this book. Mario, like many other people, grew up in the face of violent circumstance ... and yet he never places these circumstances on the centre stage of his story, which is rich with warmth and humanity. How does one explain his apparent lack of bitterness for what he has suffered? Whether it's his experiences at Boys' Town, the fact that he lived in institutions all his young life (even though both parents were alive) or the violence he endured as a routine fact of life, Mario d'Offizi treats the abusive aspects of his story with a large degree of circumspection and emotional caution. Inclined as we are to respond in absolute terms to what we perceive to be absolute issues, Mario's treatment of his story is something of a shock.

There are several angles one can take when trying to explain Mario's

Fore WORD
by Andrew K. Miller

9

as we are to respond in absolute terms to what we perceive to be absolute issues, Mario's treatment of his story is something of a shock.

There are several angles one can take when trying to explain Mario's delivery of his story. One is that a lifetime of emotional stress has forced him to detach from emotion itself; that he has been somehow divorced from the emotional stresses of his life through the force of what he endured growing up. This sounds good, and surely there must be an element of truth in it; anyone exposed to regular pain gradually develops a higher pain threshold. Whether the pain is spiritual or physical seems irrelevant to the core principal. Ultimately, however, I think this is the sort of conclusion Mario himself would treat with disdain. I think he would, instead, welcome an interpretation of his narrative that recognises that throughout his life he faced key moments, moments where his life, his journey, could have moved in any direction.

The most important of these moments was his move to Boys' Town. The alternative to Boys' Town was dire indeed, and notwithstanding the suffering he endured there, it is clear that Boys' Town had an enormous impact on his life, and that much of that impact was in fact positive. Despite his many fundamentally negative experiences, the fact remains that Mario was able to use Boys' Town as an important launch pad for the rest of his life. In Boys' Town, as in much of his life, positive and negative forces appeared in equal measures. This is surely the way of the world, and Mario demonstrates in the telling of his life story an exquisite understanding of the larger forces that balance out life as we know it. It is this understanding that, I believe, lies at the heart of this book, and that makes it as compelling as it is.

I first met Mario while I was working as the editor of a small website. It was years before we would meet in person, but within ten minutes of reading his poetry I knew that I had encountered a special writer. I was surprised, and still am, that he has managed to avoid the net of mainstream publication for so long. Over the years that I have known him, Mario has often appeared to be a person hovering on the cusp of his own life, waiting to take full ownership of it. Having experienced so much, and travelled vast distances mentally and geographically, I believe he has finally discovered his own message through the writing of his story. I believe the message he sends us, and the message he has discovered for himself, is 'Love yourself. The rest will follow.'

When you live in a continual state of conflict (and even if you don't), this is no easy maxim to digest. It demands a huge amount of patience and courage.

It has been an honour for me to work on this book. I believe it is a book that tells a particular sort of African story – the sort that is on the edge of being lost. Mario d'Offizi's generation of white South Africans was in many respects highly naïve, shrouded in the sealed cultural and emotional jar of apartheid South Africa. It is no small surprise that this generation would, and surely always will, struggle to gain any firm sense of identity, given the duplicitous sociopolitical context in which they were brought up. *Bless Me Father* is then, for me, a special adventure of self-discovery that reflects the journey either travelled or side-stepped by many white South Africans who came of age in the late sixties and seventies.

This book is a bizarre, often funny and occasionally downright joyous journey – and one wrapped up in several layers of pain. By conducting the journey as he has, Mario d'Offizi has achieved what few white South Africans of his generation have. He has looked inside himself and seen his own nakedness, his own rawness, and recognised it as a fundamental marker of human nature. He also stands by his story in the face of those who call for a more socially expected set of responses to adversity.

I salute him for it.

Andrew K. Miller
Ge'ko Publishing
March 2007

Chapter
One

After 25 years as an advertising copywriter, and a few days from my 57th birthday, I was about to attempt a change in career and embark on a journey that would forever alter my life, my thinking, and the way I saw Africa and the world.

Three years earlier I had met Matt O'Brian, a conflict journalist with many years' experience covering wars, coups and other dangerous situations in almost every country on earth. He is half Irish, just like I am. I met him by chance on Biggsy's, the dining car carriage on the Cape Town–Simons Town rail route.

On the evening trip home, drinking a few beers, my friends and I were discussing a short story I had just had published, a satirical piece about an episode I experienced during a four month stint with the South African Defence Force in Angola in early 1976.

Matt, standing in our company, was listening in. I had never seen him on the train.

Before I could say hello he introduced himself and

enquired if I was a journalist. No, an advertising copywriter, frustrated poet and short story writer, I replied. He told me a little about his background, and within ten minutes of our meeting, asked if I would be interested in joining him on an assignment in Burundi.

Matt did not waste any time. I liked that.

I was vaguely aware of what was happening in Burundi at the time. Hutus slaughtering Tutsis. Or was it the other way round?

Yes, I said, I'd love to go.

He gave me his phone number and suggested I call him to meet and talk about it. A few days later, over coffee, he told me more about conflict journalism, the countries he had been to, his experiences, and about his late partner and friend, Shaun, who had been killed in a car bomb explosion in Haifa, Israel. Matt was with Shaun when he died. Matt himself had been wounded, waking up two days later in hospital, suffering from amnesia.

The story did not deter me. I was 52, and in advertising. I was also tired of advertising. In fact, I was hanging from the cliff-face of my career by my fingertips. Remind me not to cut my nails, I joked with friends.

Matt had arranged two seats on a South African National Defence Force plane to Burundi. We were going to write stories about South African soldiers serving as peacekeepers with the United Nations, he told me. Since Christmas was around the corner, stories such as these would be warmly received, he guaranteed.

Matt and I went to Home Affairs to sort out our passports and visas. I put in for two weeks' leave. We were ready to rock, until, a few days before our departure, we were informed that we had lost our seats on the military transport plane, to two generals.

Anything for a Christmas break, Matt said sarcastically.

Matt and I stayed in contact for a while, but eventually lost touch. Three years later I was working with my son, Paul, on our little freelance set-up in Hout Street, Cape Town. Paul and I had worked together, on and off, for ten years. In October 2004, after we had both been retrenched by the ad agency we worked for – where Paul was my creative director – we formed our own business. One day, in early February 2006, Paul said to me, 'Sit down dad. I need to talk to you.' He broke the news about his decision to emigrate to New Zealand with his wife and two daughters. He was extremely concerned about me and what I would do. I had known something like this was going to happen. Paul, like me, is very impetuous and can change direction at the drop of a hat.

I took his news with composure and assured him that I would be ok, not to worry, and that he should go for it. 'Follow your heart,' I added. I always did.

Things happened quickly from there.

A few weeks earlier I had met Mike Bernardo, a South African ex-world Kick Box champion. We had discussed the idea of me helping him put his life story together, but I had no idea where to begin, no idea how to structure a biography. I just knew that, if I put my mind to it, I could pull it off. But I needed a little help. One name popped into my head: Matt O'Brian. I scratched around for Matt's number and phoned him. He admitted that he had lost my number, told me he thought my calling him at this stage was quite auspicious and mailed me pointers on the sort of basic structure I would need to get going with Mike's story.

Within a week or two of Paul's news I received a call from Matt. This time he asked me if I would like to go with him to the DRC, the Democratic Republic of Congo, to do a story about one of the DRC's most powerful Christian churches. Matt had it from good sources that the Mia Mia rebels were targeting the church and had already buried six of their pastors alive. The rebels had warned the church that their prayers were interfering with their, the rebels,' chances in the war against government troops.

We would be going to write and shoot a documentary about the church and its work in the Congo. The plan was to cut DVDs to sell in Christian fora – bookshops, churches, and hopefully to Christian television networks for broadcast. We would target the American market. The media is a giant whale. Broadcast material is the plankton on which the whale feeds. America is an ocean full of giant whales.

All I could say was that I had never used a movie camera before. Matt calmly responded that he would teach me. I made Matt promise me just one thing – that we'd be back in Cape Town for my wife Carla's 50th birthday on June 12. I would turn 57 on June 13. He gave me his word.

Three or four months before our departure, fourteen South Africans and a couple of other personnel from various other countries, 21 in all, had been arrested in the DRC on suspicion of being mercenaries planning a coup to overthrow the then government of President Joseph Kabila.

This scared me a little. But, what the hell, I thought. It's now or never. Besides, change is never easy. I thought about a saying I had once heard, which I always refer to when times are tough. Never are we nearer the light than when darkness is deepest.

On the Sunday before our departure Matt gave me a crash course on a Panasonic Mini DV video camera. We filmed boats and birds on the water at Marina Da Gama where he lives. We also went to the Sunday market at Sunrise beach, just up the road from his home, filming the stalls, the people, and anything and everything in sight. Back at his house we put a little movie together with fades, dissolves, titles and music.

A day or two before we left, I did my rounds in the city centre of Cape Town, saying goodbye to friends in coffee shops; and to our few clients. Steven Minaar, a young client service director at Ogilvy One, hugged me goodbye, placed a pink crystal in the palm of my hand, closed my fist around it, squeezed, and implored me to follow his wish:

'Promise me, Mario, that you will bury this crystal in the DRC, the Congo – for peace in Africa.' I gave him my word.

The night before we flew to Johannesburg on the first leg of our journey to the Congo, my wife, Carla, daughter, Mirella and I joined Paul and his family – his wife Leanne and my granddaughters Hannah and Kirsten – for a farewell braai.

My nephew, Paul's cousin, Wayne, and Carla's brother, Ray were with us too. This was June 1st. Paul was leaving for New Zealand on June 8th. After supper I hugged him goodbye. Paul is 35 and the last time I had heard or felt him sob was in his early teens.

Matt and his girlfriend Karen collected me at 4.30 am for the flight to Johannesburg. She dropped us at domestic departures, and after helping us unload our bags and gear, handed us a white plastic carry bag with a few magazines inside and some goodies to eat.

On the bag she had written in blue Koki:

Dear Matt & Mario

May this road take you to your destiny.
I am sure it is the start to a great adventure.

Much love, Karen

At Johannesburg airport we were met by my son Gianni and his and Paul's godfather, my best friend Carey Abdul Fanourakis. I hadn't seen either of them for nearly two years. We sat in the smoking section of the Spur Steakhouse and had beers and breakfast. I confided in Carey that I was doing this crazy trip not only as a change in career, but to become a stronger person.

Matt had the window seat. I was squeezed in the middle. A giant sat next to me in the aisle seat, dressed in khaki, deeply tanned and as rugged as Africa itself.

I have always been terrified of flying. When I do fly, I always insist on an aisle seat. Just in case. Now, stuck in the middle, squeezed uncomfortably between the two of them, I began to feel claustrophobic and unsettled. When the aircraft reached cruising height, after a smooth take-off, and we were allowed to unbuckle and stretch, I manoeuvred myself out of my seat and proceeded to the back, where the crew was preparing to serve a breakfast snack. The plane was pretty empty and I asked a steward if I could sit in one of the vacant seats.

Anywhere you like, he nodded and gestured to the empty seats left and right of the aisle.

I chose a window seat and looked out and down on terra firma. We were already crossing Zimbabwe, and the pilot informed us that Lake Kariba would soon appear beneath us. I suddenly remembered that I was scared of flying. I had never, ever before ventured to look out of the window of a plane. Nevertheless, here I was, soaring through blue, cloudless space, soaking up Kariba and the landscape north of Kariba, all of it, all the way to Lusaka, eyes glued to the scenes below me, mesmerised.

I was totally fearless and at ease. I was the heart throbbing in the metallic body of this majestic eagle in flight.

We arrived at Lusaka international airport 15 minutes ahead of schedule, disembarking and walking the short distance to the airport terminal. We collected our luggage, which included a 12 kg box of French books – *Principes*

Bibliques pour l'Afrique – which we were to deliver to the church in the Congo. I wanted to lose it a few times on our journey, but as things happened, that box played an important role in securing our safety.

We walked through the nothing-to-declare exit where an official stopped us and asked us to open the box. When he saw the content he was satisfied, and let us pass. Matt informed me that we would be met by a Pastor John Jerries, who arrived more than half an hour later with his wife Joyce and five young children. We were happy to see him, as Matt had mentioned earlier on, quite nervously, that he did not have Pastor John's cell phone number, and nor did the Pastor have his.

Pastor John greeted us warmly and enthusiastically, helped with our luggage, and loaded us into his 4x4.

He drove us to a place he had chosen for our brief stay in Lusaka, a camping site called Eureka, about 28 kilometres from the airport. We would spend the night there and he would collect us at 9.00 am the next morning, Saturday.

The children were surprisingly quiet during the journey to Eureka. I complimented Pastor John and his wife on how well behaved I thought they were. He explained that they were not his children, but orphans from the Congo. He had driven to the Congo only a few weeks earlier to collect them. Their mother had been gang-raped by government soldiers, while the children, ranging from 18 months to nine years old, and their father, had been forced to watch. When they finished with her they slit her throat and shot the father dead.

I was dazed for the rest of the journey.

We arrived at Eureka and checked into the cheapest accommodation available, a dormitory section with a few rooms, each with two single beds and a double bunk. I saw mosquito nets for the first time.

According to Matt's and my understanding, the church was going to treat us like royalty, from Zambia into the Congo and back. So we hadn't exactly brought a lot of money with us. We didn't have a lot of money to bring.

Before I left home, Carla had given me R1 000. I said I did not need it as we were going to be looked after; in fact, treated like royalty. She insisted I take it, just in case. Matt himself had only a few hundred rands.

The room at Eureka set us back about R150. We decided to skip supper.

Instead we had one local beer each. We were sipping our beers at the bar in the communal boma when two weary-looking travellers arrived to find a room. Like us, they could only afford the cheapest, the dormitory block. We introduced ourselves. They were both pastors from Mkushi, a farming community close to the Malawian border, Pastor John Symond, an ex-geography teacher from England, and Pastor Michael Tembo, a black Zambian. They both worked at an interdenominational school at Mkushi and had come to Lusaka with a 5-ton Isuzu truck to shop for mattresses, utensils and food. Since we were neighbours for the night, they invited us into their room to chat and shared their flask of coffee with us, as well as a plate of hot chips they had ordered from the kitchen.

Pastors John and Michael captivated us with their stories. They told us how happy they and the Malawian government were to have several dozen Zimbabwean farmers, thrown off their land by Robert Mugabe, developing the area. They were also intrigued by the fact that we were on our way to do a documentary about a church in the Congo.

They reminded us that it was not a safe place to visit.

Over breakfast we met a group of Canadian field workers, in Zambia doing community work with street kids. Some were trainee nurses, others teachers. All of them were Christians. We chatted a little and exchanged email addresses. One young lady, Kelly Ross, lived in Toronto, where my eldest brother David lived. The family had lost contact with him for over twenty years. I gave her my home phone number and asked her if she could pass it on to David if ever she came into contact with him, but please, not to go out of her way.

Six weeks later, back in Cape Town, I received a call just before midnight. It was David. 'I believe there are rumours that I am dead,' is how he started the conversation. We chatted a long while. Then he handed me over to speak to his fourth wife, whom he had recently married. Her name was Carla.

The field workers were also intrigued by our trip to the Congo. They wished us a safe journey.

As promised, Pastor John arrived to collect us just after 9.00 am. We drove a short way to his house, or rather, the orphanage, the Samaritan Children's Home, where he and Joyce lived with 53 orphans. There could be a lot more children here, Pastor John told us. Every day they had to turn children away. There were just too many homeless, too many orphans for one couple to feed and care for. Pastor John and his church, the Every Nation Church, fed up to 6 000 children daily, throughout Zambia and in southern Congo. The orphanage was a work in progress, he explained as he proudly showed us around the place. For Pastor John and Joyce there was a pastor's office, a small bedroom en-suite, and a little lounge. And for the children there were a few little bedrooms, each with two double bunks. There was a communal room and a kitchen, where Joyce cooked three meals a day for her children. Outside, a school building, clinic, conference centre and another dormitory block were taking shape. Pastor John explained that they were building the conference centre so that they could hire it out to help sustain the orphanage and the children.

Our work started in earnest.

Armed with our cameras, we captured the children at prayer and at play. They sang for us. They danced and clapped, in the name of Jesus. 'Jesus!' The children refrained. I cried a little inside.

Matt set up the tripod and camera in Pastor John's office.

Pastor John took up his seat behind his desk, and as Matt had taught me, I rigged the mike to his jacket lapel. Then Matt placed the headphones on me and nonchalantly whispered, 'You're doing this interview. Just remember the rule of thirds. Don't centre your subject.' Then he left the room.

I was a little nervous at first, but when Pastor John began to speak, about love for God's work, about how it's all about the children, my confidence grew. I had never ever felt such passion and compassion emanating from another human being.

Bless you, bless you, Father John. Bless you, Mother Joyce.

My mother's name was also Joyce. She had 13 pregnancies. Nine births and four miscarriages, from her first two husbands. All of us children were either fostered or went to orphanages and children's homes.

Pastor John was taking me back on a long road.

* * *

Alba sat on the swing and Lillian and I pushed her and we were singing that song, 'Don't sell Daddy any more Whiskey.' Leandro played in the dirt in our tiny, flower-bare, shrub-bare backyard. There was a single big pepper tree. The swing was a wooden plank strung to the tree by a rope.

We pushed Alba higher and higher until she screamed.

We didn't notice Leandro, lying on the ground, writhing and convulsing, until Alba saw what was happening and her screams took on a piercing shrill 'LEE! LEEE! LEEE! LEANDRO is dying ... STOP!'

'Shut up Alba,' Lillian hollered, 'You're screaming so loud you're gonna wake mommy from her nap and there's gonna be all hell to pay, and Mario and me are the ones who will get the buckle and belt.' But our mother was already outside, bent over Lee and fiddling in his mouth, shouting, 'Lillian! Mario! Go fetch a bloody spoon, hurry before this child swallows his tongue!'

Lillian ran to the house and back in a flash with a tablespoon.

Alba couldn't stop screaming and our mother yelled at her 'SHUT UP! SHUT UP!' I just stood there, frozen to the ground. Alba didn't shut up and Lillian smacked her across the face. She fled into the house. If our father came home drunk that night, like he mostly did, with that terrible temper of his, he would have blamed Lillian and me. Because we were the oldest. Lillian was just nine months older than me, I was eight, Alba was five and Leandro was only eighteen months. Leandro was the apple of his eye, and as he grew up he became even more so. Only Leandro, in time to come, would be allowed to buy sweets and cold drinks on tick at Rose's corner café.

Our father came home drunk that night but mother didn't say a word about that day's episode. She had warned us not to say anything either, because you never knew with him.

Early one evening my father sent me to Rose's Café to buy a loaf of bread, and on my way back a black man stopped me. He was cupping a little bird with a broken wing in his hands. I felt sorry for the little bird, and the man gave it to me. I gave him the loaf of bread.

I skipped all the way home sort of singing – shouting, 'I'm Mario d'Offizi, I'm Mario d'Offizi and I saved a little bird! I saved a little bird!' When I got home I was proud and excited so I went to show the little bird to my father.

'Where's the bread?'

When I told him that I swapped the bread for the bird the veins began to swell in his forehead and he swore and beat me about the head. I ran across the road into the grounds of Rose Lodge, the boarding house, to hide from him.

My mother screamed at him, telling him she swore that if he hurt me she'd call welfare and the police.

I hid in the long grass in the orchard at the boarding house. It was a warm, clammy dusk and the light was fading. I saw my father in brownish shorts and a white sleeveless vest, with his pocket-knife in his hands. He studied the branches of a quince tree, sizing them up.

He broke a branch from the tree. He was whistling then, a familiar song like *Arri-vi-der-ci Ro-o-ma*, as he deftly worked the blade, cleaning the branch of its bark. Fondling the smooth cane lovingly, like it was a woman, and whistling on, he stalked me.

The bedside stories he told us kids were about the war in Abyssinia. We laughed at his funny accent. Our father was Italian and I once heard a man call him a fucking eyetie prisoner of war. My father beat him to a pulp. The police came and it took quite a lot of them to put him in the back of their van. He knew all about war and killing, and with his soldier's instincts he stalked me, knowing exactly in which direction I moved.

I didn't realise it at the time, but not only was he stalking me, he was also shepherding me into the large dining room of the boarding house. Because that's where I ended up, under a table in the far corner from the front door. That's where he captured me, and with equal lashings from his feet and the quince cane, he beat me.

My mother did what she had threatened to. She called the police. They took him away that night, but he was back the next day.

Within a few days the welfare people came and took Lillian, Alba and me back to the children's home in Kimberley, about a hundred miles from our home in Bloemfontein. That's where we spent our Christmas. Again. Because Leandro was only eighteen months old, they left him behind.

But we knew, then, that it was just a matter of time before he joined us.

It was also only a matter of time before all three of my siblings were to die young and tragically.

First Leandro, followed a year later by Lillian, and then Alba.

Leandro was 24. Lillian was 31 and Alba, 48.

* * *

Close to 11.00 am Pastor John dropped a little bombshell. His vehicle had been damaged, and it would never make the 500 or so kilometers to the Congo border. Besides, he didn't have a re-entry visa to take us through the border post. He had been on the phone to other pastors, but there were no vehicles available, and nobody to drive us. There was only one daily bus to Chililabombwe, the northernmost town in Zambia. It left from the main bus terminus in the city centre. With urgency, we set out for town to find a bank so that Matt could change some rands into Kwacha and dollars for the journey. Before we left the orphanage — lunch had been cooked for the children — we each grabbed a few handfuls of rice. We ate our handfuls without milk, sugar or gravy.

At a shopping centre close to the bus terminus we met a Pastor Vicky, a young man who was Bishop Lamba Lamba's son, and another church worker. They were on their cellphones, trying to organise a lift for us.

No joy.

It was then I first heard Matt use the acronym, AWA.

I asked him to explain. He said that it was a word we would often use on our journey. It was journalese-speak used by that fellowship of conflict journalists, called OAHs, Old Africa Hands. It was a cry of resignation. A chant in anger. AWA. Africa Wins Again.

Pastor John then phoned Bishop Lamba Lamba, informing him that we would be bussing up, staying the night at Chililabombwe, and that we would be at the border when it opened at 8.00 am the next morning.

And please to send somebody to meet us.

The terminus bustled like a busy marketplace. Bedlam. Throngs of travellers piling into and out of buses. Everybody trying to sell us tickets, to God knows

24

where. Confusing. Pastor Vicky took money from Matt to buy our tickets, suspecting that we ourselves might get ripped off; the others helped load our bags and the box of bible-books onto the packed bus.

We had to climb over piles of suitcases and other luggage clogging the aisle to get to our seats towards the very back of the bus. There were satellite dishes leaning out of windows. Above our heads, a double bed mattress was slung and fastened between the luggage racks. We had just made the bus on time, the only one to Chililabombwe that day.

We were both mindful of our dwindling money supply. The fares were R100 each, or 100 000 Kwacha. We also had most of our luggage stored on our laps.

The bus set off on what is called the Great North Road.

After about three hours we stopped at the first town en route, Kabwe, where we got out stretching and had a much needed smoke break. I had been sitting by the window and my left side and kidneys were aching.

Matt had been squeezed alongside me in the aisle seat and his right side and kidneys were aching. When we got back on the bus we swapped seats.

The people were very friendly and I made light conversation with a few.

'How long to Chililabombwe?'

'About 6 hours.'

'When and where is the next stop?' I was craving another cigarette.

'Ndola, then Kitwe, Chingola and Chililabombwe. But we can only get off at Kitwe for a short break.'

'Thanks.'

Matt was reading some war novel, a Vietnam story. When he noticed that I was becoming increasingly bored and frustrated, he pulled out the three magazines Karen had included in her white plastic goodies bag. There were also four meat sticks, which we shared. I spread the magazines on my lap. One was the *New African*, with a cover story about the origins of the ancient Egyptians. The other two were scary.

Time Magazine, June 5, 2006. A silhouette of a despairing-looking Congolese boy, with the headline: CONGO. THE HIDDEN TOLL OF THE WORLD'S DEADLIEST WAR. The other was *BBC Focus on Africa*, April-June 2006. A picture of Joseph Kabila on the cover. The caption: KABILA'S CONGO ... LOOTERS' PARADISE.

'You've got a fucking dark sense of humour, you bastard.' He just winked at me, and smiled. 'Nothing wrong with doing a bit of homework, is there?'

I only started reading quite a bit later.

Zambians are very friendly and proud to be a Christian nation. If South Africa is the powerhouse from which Africa's economic, political and cultural renaissance is supposedly to be launched, then Zambia could well become the altar from which Africa's spiritual revival may spring. I struck up a short conversation with the young man sitting across the narrow aisle, next to me. He told me he was a pastor from Chingola and gave me his details.

'My friend here, alongside me, and I are going to the DRC to do a documentary about a Christian church.'

'I am proud to be travelling with servants of God.'

I felt like a missionary. The Zambian sunset was refreshing. Warm light flashed through the windows of the speeding bus. I saw a red orb sink into the mouth of the wide and hungry western horizon.

At every stop on the way, the bus emptied a little. Between the last two stops, Chingola and Chililabombwe, the rear half of the bus was empty. Matt and I went right to the back, opened the windows, and like schoolboys, indulged in a few sneaky smokes.

We arrived in Chililabombwe just after 8.00 pm. As we climbed off the bus, we were badgered by taxi drivers.

We were tired and in no mood to barter, and in no position to. We were, in fact, in completely foreign territory. We settled for a driver wearing a floppy white hat and asked him to take us to the cheapest B&B there was. He did.

Sadly, he also ripped us off. I anticipated it on our way to the B&B, when he said, 'I am taking a short cut.'

He dropped us off at Dreams B&B. On arrival, he hooted at the gate and an elderly man, the night watchman, opened for us.

'The owner is in bed recovering, and I will take care of you both. You can make payment to the owner tomorrow morning,' he assured us. The driver hit us for 50 000 Kwacha — the same price as a single bus ticket from Lusaka to Chililabombwe. Matt called him a robber, but we had no choice but to cough up. We did not know the cost of taxi fares in Zambia. We did know that we had been severely conned. AWA.

We had been informed that the border was less than an hour's drive from Chililabombwe. We took the driver's cell number and asked him to collect us at 6.45 am the next day, urging him to be on time. We were shown to our room. Two three-quarter beds. Clean, crisp linen. Bedside table with lamp. Tray, with glasses and flask of water. We were warned not to drink water from taps.

Only boiled water would do in this part of the world. More especially in the Congo, the night watchman added, after we mentioned that we were on our way there. Matt said not to worry. He had, in his survival kit, enough water purification tablets to last us to Cairo.

It was too late to eat — besides, there was no one to cook for us — so we showered and prepared for bed. There was a TV set in the room. We asked the man if they had DSTV. 'Yes,' he said. We asked if he could switch to channel 21. That afternoon the Springbok rugby side had played a World XV. The highlights were scheduled for much, much later. Off with the TV. We smoked a little and chatted about the trip so far. We said nothing about the morrow, except to get up early, have a good breakfast, and make sure to get to the border on time.

After all, our hosts from the Congo would be waiting for us.

We woke up a little before 6.00 am. Our hostess, Lizzie, a lovely, sprightly lady with a hearing aid and excellent English, was up to greet and welcome us. She apologised for not being there to meet us the night before, explaining that she had just returned from hospital after suffering a bout of malaria. Lizzie offered to cook breakfast and we sat down on the porch outside to coffee, scrambled eggs with toast, baked beans, fried tomato and peanut butter. Made in Zambia.

We told her how much our fare to her guest house had cost us, and she swore she would report the driver to the police. The fare should have only cost us 6 000 Kwacha. We described the driver and his car. Don't worry, she promised, she would sort him out. Lizzie phoned another taxi driver, a great guy with the unlikely name McIver, to pick us up in the morning and take us to the border town of Kasumbalesa. He played Bob Marley and UB40's "Red, Red Wine" in the car. I complimented him on his choice of music.

On our approach to the border there were hundreds of trucks lined up on either side of the road, stretching for at least eight kilometres. McIver explained that they were waiting for the border to open and that they were transporting food, clothing, machinery and other goods to the Congo. There were also trucks laden with cars and 4-wheel-drive vehicles.

The Sainsbury's truck stood out. Emblazoned on its side: SAINSBURY'S. WHERE GOOD FOOD TASTES BETTER.

When we stopped at the border and McIver opened the boot, three youngsters, Fagin's urchins, appeared, grabbed our luggage and carried it two metres from the car. They were angry when Matt gave them 1 000 Kwacha, about R2.

The smallest of the three looked Matt up and down with contempt and demanded more money.

We told him in good South African slang where to go.

They left. But not without stealing Matt's pillow from his backpack.

We waited outside the doors of Zambian Customs while a female official in uniform swept the floor, the dust billowing out. The Zambian officials were extremely courteous. A female official stared at Matt with amazement.

'Are you going to DR Congo?'

Matt nodded.

'You crazy!'

With our passports stamped and in order, we walked the 500 or so metres across no-man's-land to DRC Customs. As we stepped onto DRC soil we were confronted by three officials in jeans, coloured shirts, with holstered pistols and rifles. They led us into a holding pen consisting of a number of creosote poles topped with a tin roof and a floor of cow-dung. Sitting on a stool was a man with one-way dark glasses, a multi-coloured bandana and an evil mood about him. He told us to put our luggage down in front of him. He indicated a spot at his feet. He sized us up.

Who are we? What are we doing in the DRC? Where are we headed?

He spoke in broken English.

'I am special intelligence for President Joseph Kabila.'

We explained that we were in the DRC by invitation of Bishop Lamba Lamba of the Come and See Church. We pointed out the box of French books as proof.

I was shaking at the knees. My mouth was dead, my heart beat furiously and I was almost blinded by fear.

He pointed to our luggage.

'10 dollar each and we no search your luggage.'

We told him he was free to search our luggage.

'You give 20 dollars.'

We swore we had no money. I asked him if he took rands. At first he said no. I then took out my wallet, opened it, and turning away to hide the few hundred rands inside, gave him ten rand. Suddenly one of his henchmen noticed Matt's camera bag. He shrieked.

'Do you have camera? No camera! No camera!'

I thought about the camera in my backpack.

Matt was quick and firm. 'President Joseph Kabila gave me permission to bring a camera to do an interview with Bishop Lamba Lamba. And the embassy in Pretoria gave permission too.' He lied with a straight face. He also reluctantly handed over $20.

The official calmed down. Situation diffused.

They let us move on. But only to make us sweat a little.

After we passed other officials to have our passports stamped, all of them wanting dollars we did not really have, apart from the last twenty Matt had on him, two heavily-armed soldiers appeared, took Matt by the arms and led him to a military outpost near the holding pen.

I stood, confused and frightened, in what seemed like the middle of nowhere, with soldiers and police grabbing at the books. I told them we were in the Congo to meet Bishop Lamba Lamba. I told anybody interested that we were missionaries. That we had no money. The name Lamba Lamba was greeted with respect and in some instances with what seemed like awe. An older official, in blue police uniform, took a few books for his family. He asked me for money. I told him that the others had taken it all. He shrugged.

Meanwhile, the soldiers extracted our last 20 dollars from Matt at gunpoint.

A soldier held a rifle to his head. When Matt handed over our dollars he asked for a receipt. The soldier holding the gun to his head cocked the rifle.

My nerves were jumping all over the place, scattered in the ominous wind that had risen.

A policeman finally unlocked the gates and we walked into Kasumbalesa. And into the jaws of hell. Matt said Dante must have had a vision of Kasumbalesa before he wrote The Inferno. The wind lifted and dust, smelly dust, red like dried blood, whirled about us. We managed to smile at each other. We were expecting somebody from the Come and See Church to meet us, to take us to safety and comfort. It was impossible for them not to recognise us.

During the chaos in our crossing into the Congo, we met a black South African, travelling from Johannesburg to visit his family. He said he was taking a taxi to Lubumbashe and that we should think about traveling with him. He told us Kasumbalesa was a very dangerous place, with dangerous people. A whorehouse and a smugglers' den. I looked down the long road, with stalls, shacks and broken down old houses lining a cavernous, pot-holed track which was the main road. Chickens, goats, pigs and piglets moved in and amongst the throng of people. There were hundreds of trucks lining both sides of the road. These, Matt suggested, were probably transporting the riches of the Congo – minerals and other valuables – to the rest of the world.

We agreed I would stay near the border gate and watch our gear while he walked down the road to find our hosts. Hopefully.

It was one of the longest passages of my long life. Fear and panic set in. Matt had explained to me on the plane that our journey would be a hectic roller coaster ride. I started to understand his meaning.

One moment you experience relief and joy. The very next, knee-knocking fear.

While Matt was away a young man, dressed in a smart grey suit with a bright red shirt, a red, blue and yellow tie and pointy black patent leather shoes, stopped to greet me. He seemed surprised at my standing there alone. He asked who I was, what I was doing and introduced himself as Pastor Enoch. I hugged him.

'Are you from Bishop Lamba Lamba to meet us?'

'No.' He was taken aback.

'I am a pastor travelling from Harare, Zimbabwe, where I work and live. I am on my way to spend a month with my Congolese wife and my children in Lubumbashe.'

The roller coaster spiralled downwards. My heart followed, a heavy stone sinking to the bottom of a muddy lake.

As I was explaining our situation to Pastor Enoch, Matt returned saying that he had not seen anyone from the church and that we were really in trouble. I introduced him to Pastor Enoch, who told us that he had been on his way to the end of the road, to find a taxi, when God suddenly told him to go back to the border gates. Now he knew without doubt that God had sent him to find us, he said.

He was the first of a few angels to walk with us over the next four days in the Congo.

Chapter
Two

'Our Nonna mourned for your father, Lello, from the day he left home here in Palestrina until the day she died,' Emmanuella told me.

Emmanuella is my cousin, and I was visiting my father's birthplace, Palestrina, a small, ancient town about 50 kilometres east of Rome. It was a Sunday family lunch with family I had never seen before. A large, festive and noisy gathering.

We sat at an enormous table in a special cooking and eating area attached to the house of my aunt, Zia Amadea, my father's only sister. He had five brothers, and Emmanuella, daughter of my father's eldest brother Lorenzo – dead by now – was the only one who could speak English; albeit broken English. I was sitting opposite her. I asked her to tell me about my father; perhaps I would learn of things I did not know.

'Your father left home when he was very young, he was sixteen ... he was sent with Mussolini's soldiers, they called them Black Shirts ... to Africa, to Abyssinia to fight, even before the Second World War.' I knew my father had served in North and East Africa from a very young age. 'Until the day she died, Nonna mourned for your father, and she would not give up hope that he would return home one day. She would not allow anybody into your father's room. She loved Zio Lello, your father. Once a week she would change the sheets and put a fresh glass of wine, some bread and a piece of cheese on the table beside his bed. Every week, until she died, 27 years after your father left Palestrina. For 27 years she put the bread and wine and cheese out for him. But she never saw your father after he left Palestrina. He was her youngest child and the one she did not want to go to war ... she loved all her children ... my father, Lorenzo, but Zio Lello, your father, was very special for her.'

My father only returned to Italy in 1967. Financially he did not have the means to go back earlier. He battled most of his life; six days of the week.

I looked through the large window behind where Emmanuella was seated, and stared at the olive trees and grape vines in the garden, imagining my father picking grapes and olives and immersing himself in the flowers and the vegetables and the creatures of the garden, revelling in his family close by, eating pasta and drinking wine.

Emmanuella translated for other members of the family. Little anecdotes emerged about Nonna and my grandfather, and how he had died mysteriously – they swore to that day that it was murder. The excitement grew, gesticulations became more and more animated and expressive ... little debates surfaced, the

Italian passion flowing with the wines, all home-made, delicious whites and reds, made by Zio Amerigo himself. Zia Amadea's husband, who was 92 then, kept a cellar in the garden.

Every now and then, throughout the lunch, Zio Amerigo would take me by the arm and we would go to the cellar to fetch more wine. The cellar was deceptive. It looked like a large dog's kennel, but built of bricks, and after opening the door and stooping through the entrance, one would go deep into the ground, down stone steps; the deeper you descended, the colder it became. The whites were kept down below to chill; the reds were at the upper levels. There was an endless supply and variety of pasta served, lamb and other meats, grilled in a stone oven in the room by Zia Amadea, who did not have to leave her seat to turn the meat, the oven was so close to her. We enjoyed freshly baked breads, salads – home-grown greens and tomatoes – and olives from Zio Amerigo's precious trees in the garden. And the love and laughter were infectious.

This Sunday was a family feast to welcome me and Carla on our visit to Palestrina. I learnt then how proud my family was of Palestrina and its history. They were not too fond of the Romans, though. My cousin Renzo, Emmanuella's eldest brother, told me through Emmanuella that Palestrina was previously known as Antica Preneste and was almost two thousand years older than Rome itself. The Romans had besieged Palestrina for over a thousand years before finally conquering it and its people – who still considered the Romans inferior. It was renamed sometime in the 14th century. I verified these facts in a brochure I picked up at Palestrina's world-famous museum on the outskirts of the town, at the foothills of a small mountain, on top of which is San Pietro, a tiny, charming village, with a baker who made the best breads I've ever eaten. I saw an old man, a young boy and a few dogs shepherd a flock of sheep off the grassland of the mountain and down a narrow road through San Pietro. A few of the sheep wore little bells about their necks, and the tinkling of these, along with their bleating and the sounds of their trotting, momentarily blended with the pealing of the 6.00 pm church bells.

I was in an environment so warm and loving I became sad during that lunch, mostly because I thought about how my father had been taken away from this home and family at such a young age. How different his life would have been had he stayed. And how different the lives of his children. I had only heard and read about how closely-knit, and extended, Italian families were. Now I felt it, was part of it. I wished then that my father could be there, together with us.

Of all the stories and little family anecdotes I heard during my brief stay in

Palestrina, Emmanuella's story about Nonna and her dedicated weekly ritual of hope, love, bread and wine and cheese, was the most poignant and indelible. It made me wonder a little about my own upbringing, and that of my brother and sisters, and my mother and father's divorce. Some of the things I regretted were that I had not had the opportunity to learn Italian; and the fact that my father had naturalised and become a South African citizen when I was fifteen and a minor. Had he waited until after my 18th birthday I would automatically have had rights to an Italian passport.

Despite the fact that we children all landed up in children's homes, and all of us, my mother included, were often subjected to his violent outbursts (I had many a hiding, especially when he drank), I never resented him. I always used the excuse that the war had affected him. So many years in North Africa, living the wild, reckless and often lonely life of a soldier, had desensitised him. Because there were times, when he opened his armour just a little, that I saw a compassionate, kind and loving man.

Once, a few months before he died, when I, Carla and the children where visiting him at his home in Munster on the South Coast, and I was alone with him in his chicken-run (his chickens loved him and would crowd on his shoulders, even sit on his head), he suddenly started crying softly and, hugging me, apologising for being a bad father and for how we had suffered growing up. And that he had never been there for us.

'It wasn't your fault, Dad,' I said. 'You came here as a prisoner of war, you could barely speak English … you didn't have a proper chance.' I really meant it. I told him to shed the guilt; that we loved him as a father. Unlike our Nonna, I was able and grateful to be with him almost to the end of his life.

My father was a very popular man and had many friends. He was a builder and skilled stonemason who built many of the first homes in Munster. His home was practically on the beach. He grew bananas, vegetables, fruit trees, and kept chickens and ducks. He even had a few pigs at one stage – they used to stroll with him down to the beach in the evenings and bathe with him in the rock pools.

But he was hard on us, especially on me, his eldest son. When I came home once a year for holidays, always over Christmas, he made me work from early morning until about 4.00 pm each day. I would carry, stack and un-stack rocks and bricks, mix cement and help with the building. I hated it. Especially since I was on holiday and my friends were on the beach and having fun. I knew not to resist or argue with him, though. A short man, he was nonetheless powerful and had enormous hands and a 56-inch barrel chest. My mother always mocked his bandy legs. By now he had stopped drinking and even attended Alcoholics Anonymous meetings. For the rest of his life he was a recovering alcoholic.

It was during these times that I learned about his time in the army. While we worked together, he would tell me his stories from Abyssinia and Eritrea.

He was sent there in 1928 and remained there until his capture by South African forces in Kenya in 1943, when he was brought to South Africa and interned in a prisoner of war camp at Sonderwater. After the war he was sent to work as a labourer on a farm near Bloemfontein. He told me how he had saved a pilot from the burning wreck of an Italian fighter plane near Addis Ababa. How he had taken refuge in a large pool of water encircled by reeds to escape from the extremely dangerous Afar freedom fighters (then known as Danakil 'terrorists'), and survived the search by staying under water and breathing through a home-made schnorkel cut from a reed shaft.

And how he had amputated the leg of a young Arabian boy in a primitive field hospital at Hargeisa. In the absence of the hospital surgeon and assisted by two nuns, he undertook the amputation of the critically advanced, gangrenous leg without any anaesthetics.

The nuns had earlier warned him not to perform the operation and had threatened to report him to the authorities. My father told me that he took the risk mostly because he could no longer bear the child's suffering and the pleas of the father. There were no anaesthetics, so he struck the boy unconscious with a blow to the cheek.

He had no other choice. Towards the end of the operation, while he was stitching the leg he told me that the boy woke up, smiled at him ('he smiled like a little angel') and then lost consciousness again.

My father was commended for his successful surgery by the surgeon on his return to the hospital a few days later. It was this amputation of the young Arabian boy's leg that inspired my father's friend, Professor Johan Bekker of the University of Potchefstroom, who lived at Glenmore Beach nearby, to write a 'faction' novel based on my father's wartime experiences. The book was written in Afrikaans and published in the early 1980s by Perskor, entitled: *Ranke Wat Uitstoot* (Roots that Spread Out). There is a photograph of my father on the first page with the caption: *Lello, mio amigo.* At the end of the book, Johan Bekker tells how he visited Palestrina and how he had conducted his research at the War Museum in Rome to verify the facts.

My father had in his possession three medals and a hand-written citation with Mussolini's original signature. Not mentioned in the book were a few other experiences my father told me.

Like the fact that in the fifteen years he was there he had four 'concubines,' as he put it. I can only imagine how many brothers and sisters, nephews, nieces and cousins I have living in the region. That is, those who have survived the terrible turmoil and succession of wars that have plagued it since then.

He also told me how he had originally come to be at the field hospital at Hargeisa. He had been captured by the Afar (Danakil) 'terrorists' who were fighting against the colonisation of their country by Italy. They stripped him naked, tied him to a tree and greased him with a sweet substance to attract insects and flies. The Danakils would do this to their Italian prisoners for a few days. Then they would castrate them, put their testicles in their mouths, sew their lips tightly together and drop them near Italian positions as a warning to the rest of the Italian soldiers.

During his second night in captivity an old lady, who had been watching him closely during the time he was tied up, pointed to the large silver crucifix he was wearing. He told me that she offered to let him loose in exchange for the crucifix. He agreed, and later that night she untied him, brought him some clothes and a donkey and sent him off in the direction of the nearest Italian positions. When he arrived at an Italian base, the Commanding Officer did not believe his story. He accused my father of being a deserter and a coward. This angered Lello D'Ofizzi, who grabbed a bayonet from a soldier standing alongside the Commanding Officer, and stabbed him in the stomach. Lello was arrested and court-martialled. He won the desertion case but was found guilty of assault, stripped of his rank (Sergeant-Major) and sent to the field hospital for six months as a male nurse and cleaner. Somehow the stabbing and the amputation of the young boy's leg reminded me of an incident my mother had told me about my father when they lived together in their early days.

He was working late one weekend on a building site when he was hit in the mouth by a steel girder, which broke a few of his teeth. She said that he was in such agony the night it happened that, after drinking almost an entire bottle of brandy, he took out a pair of pliers and wrenched at least five teeth out, including molars. On the Monday he went to a dentist, had the rest extracted and had dentures made.

One story my father related to me intrigued me for many, many years. One day, when I was about 17, again on holiday and working with him as usual, he asked me – out of the blue – if I had ever heard of or tried marijuana 'dagga'. I felt maybe he suspected I was smoking it. I said yes I knew of it, and defensively assured him that I had never smoked it.

He told me that in about 1931 in Abyssinia – now known as Ethiopia – he used to accompany a young prince on night hunting trips. They would specifically hunt leopards, he said. And he would often smoke marijuana with the prince and his entourage. A few years ago I went onto the internet to find out more about Ethiopia. There was a young prince living there in 1931 who became Emperor in 1932. His name was Haile Selassie.

* * *

'Lolly! That fucking bitch lollipop took my husband, your father ... away from me and from you children ... she stole him, the bitch!' I heard this often from my mother. She was bitter about Lolly. At first I was too young to understand it, because Aunty Lolly had always been very kind to me, although she was quite a cold, aloof woman. She was a miser when it came to money and would only buy what was absolutely necessary. She was far, far richer than us.

My father had an affair with Lolly when I was very young, which led to my parents' divorce. I was complicit in this affair at times, but in an innocent way. On a few occasions – during my holidays home, when my parents still lived in Bloemfontein – my father would tell my mother that he wanted to spend time alone with me and take me to the drive-in. He would pick Lolly up, and I would watch the movie from the brick building, the projection room, where cool drinks and burgers were sold, next to the rows of parked cars. My father would watch the movies alone with Lolly in the car. That's if they ever watched the movies. He would tell me exactly what to tell my mother, because she always asked. I was terrified to tell her the truth.

One holiday, when I came home from Nazareth House, my father was living alone in a boarding house. My mother was living with another man somewhere else; also in a boarding house. She introduced me to Uncle Henry. He had one leg and we later on called him 'Peg-leg.' Soon after, she and Henry moved to Hillbrow in Johannesburg.

When Lolly's husband died, she was left a comfortable amount of money and she and my father moved into a big house in one of Bloemfontein's 'better' suburbs. She had one son, Cedric, who stayed with them and was given the best of everything. I only spent one holiday a year with them. I liked Cedric, but thought that he was pretty spoilt. We became friends of a kind.

One holiday I came home and was put to work in my father's and Lolly's fish and chip shop, opposite the library and museum. It was called Oranje Fish & Chips. I was about thirteen. I used to scrub potatoes and put them through the chip cutter, clean and help wash dishes, and accompany my father to the local market to buy fresh fruit and vegetables. He caught me one day giving free fish to a beggar and gave me a clout to the cheek that almost knocked me off my feet – in front of other customers in the shop.

I found out by accident one day that my father was selling liquor under the counter. A man walked in and asked for a bunch of bananas. My father had gone out on an errand and I was alone in the shop with his assistant, Mrs. Muller, who was attending to other customers. I told the man we did not sell bananas. He smiled at me and said he'd wait for Mrs. Muller. Mrs. Muller told the man to wait for Lello; he'd be back in a few minutes. When my father returned he greeted the man warmly, went to the storeroom in the back and placed a bottle of brandy in a brown paper bag.

My father, I came to learn, was very careful. And wily. One Saturday night, it was late and I was tired, anxious to go home, a man walked in and spoke to my father. My father went to the back to the store room and returned with a bottle in a brown paper bag. The man left and returned a few minutes later, with a few other men. They were detectives. They turned the place upside down, but could not find a drop of alcohol. They arrested my father. When he asked them to give me a lift home, one of them swore at him and told him that I could walk. My father locked the shop, gave me the house keys, and I walked home. It took a few hours.

Aunty Lolly was away visiting relatives with Cedric, and my father and I were alone in the house. I saw my father again late the following Monday. He told me later that he had been tipped off by a policeman friend of his and had sold the detective a bottle of brandy – without the brandy. He had refilled the bottle with strong black tea.

When he went to court on the Monday morning, he pointed this out to the magistrate. He was given a warning; the case was thrown out due to lack of

39

evidence. The detective who had been embarrassed carried out a vendetta against my father and would raid the shop at all hours. But my father was never caught again.

A year or two later I received a letter from Aunt Lolly informing me that she and my father had moved to Munster on the South Coast of Natal. I looked forward to future holidays when I read that letter. I had never seen the sea.

At almost the same time my mother, married by now to Uncle Henry, had sent me a letter informing me that they had moved to Cape Town.

During my last year at Boys' Town, Father Orsmond told me one day that Lady Ina Oppenheimer had offered to buy a piece of land on the coast to build a holiday camp for Boys' Town. And that they had chosen Munster and were in discussion with my father about the building and maintenance of the camp.

There was great excitement in the small local community. The South Coast Herald reported that Lady Caroline 'Ina' Oppenheimer and Father Reginald Orsmond had had tea with Lello and Lolly d'Offizi to discuss building plans; and that Lello d'Offizi had been awarded the building contract. After completing the building of the camp, named Camp Carolina after Lady Oppenheimer, my father was appointed caretaker. He was caretaker until just before his death and was affectionately known by the boys, the teachers and Father Orsmond, as Mr. Dof.

In this time he taught Father Orsmond the basics of Italian cooking; especially their favourite, spaghetti Bolognese. I heard that often over the years, when the boys and teachers travelled from Magaliesberg to Munster, they would arrive tired, weary and hungry to a feast of spaghetti Bolognese. They loved my father for this.

When he died, the South Coast Herald reported his death as a loss to the Munster community and to Boys' Town particularly.

Life has its ironies.

Chapter
Three

One day, while we were holidaying at Munster on the South Coast, my father bought chocolates for my children, Paul, Gianni and Gabriella. He held the sweets out in his hands and invited the children to choose. They rushed to him. Paul, being the oldest, was there first and grabbed the biggest chocolate of the three. My father cuffed him on the ear, took the chocolate back and handed it to Gabriella. He gave Gianni one, and put the last one back in his pocket, denying Paul, who fled the scene in tears.

I took my father aside and quietly berated him about the incident. He gave me the argument that the youngest, especially a girl, should have first choice. I was in no mood to argue, and for the sake of peace, let the matter be. But it hurt. It really, really hurt. A quiet anger rose inside me as I recalled all the violence I had experienced at my father's hands during my childhood. I took Paul aside and consoled him. I used the excuse that grandpa had been brought up like this. Violence was the only language he understood. I told Paul about the tough life his grandpa had lived, and fell back on the disclaimer that it was too late to change old, deep-rooted habits. Paul wasn't stupid. He was ten years old. He broke away from me, crying and swearing: 'I hate fucking grandpa. He's not my grandpa!' All I could do was sigh and hope that Paul would forget and forgive. He never did. He has never forgotten this incident. Nor has he forgiven his grandfather. Over the years Paul has felt a fascination and even a form of admiration for the man. But forgive? Or forget? Never.

I can never forget my childhood. But I do forgive. I think it is simply my nature to do so. Many of my friends and relatives think I'm crazy. Especially Paul. I have taken pains over the years to explain to Paul, and my other children, that bitterness only serves to make us bitter. If we hold onto it we achieve no more than slowly killing ourselves.

Many years after the chocolate incident, when Paul and I started to work together, I felt the time had come for me to confide in him about my past. After all, we were now in an adult relationship, and we were business partners. We sometimes reversed roles and I would ask advice from him – as if I were his son. He often joked that he should be charging me psychologist's consultation fees. When I told him about my experiences at the hands of his grandpa, and especially my relationship with Father Orsmond, he said, 'Jeez dad, I would have killed the fuckers ... can understand grandpa, just a bit, but not the other shit. No way.'

Carla had said, so often, to me, 'Break the chain ... break the chain.' No matter how the children infuriated me from time to time, I controlled my temper and especially that thoughtless, inherent urge to lash out; to give them 'the hiding of their life.'

Only once did I lash out at Paul – with a soft, controlled kick to his buttocks. I felt incredible guilt and remorse for a long time afterwards. He still jokes that it was the biggest 'no hiding' he ever received from me.

The power of father figures slowly and subtly became apparent to me in later years – I started to notice a rather strange, if not weird, phenomenon. At first it bothered me, and reminded me of a form of schizophrenia, the thought of which had haunted me in my youth. I became intrigued by this and would actually – with a strange sense of detachment – observe and study my behaviour.

The phenomenon is this: When I found myself in an intellectual, cultural or social debate, I would take on the mannerisms of Father Orsmond. Just like Father Orsmond, I would hold my cigarette between my fingers and without gesticulating, rest the elbow of my left arm (the one holding the cigarette) in the palm of my right arm ... and listen to the debate pensively and thoughtfully before offering my opinions. I would use the phrase 'always take the consequences of your actions ...' if it was called for. Even today, at times I can hear his voice resonating softly along with mine. If two people faced each other in a stand-off I would intervene with the utmost diplomacy and tact.

However, if I was in a debate that stirred my passions, I would gesticulate like my father, waving my arms and hands about, passionately getting my point across. If a stand-off between belligerents erupted into violence, I would get between the protagonists and forcefully attempt to separate them. My fathers, for better or worse, have shaped me. They are still with me today. There is no shaking that fact. When I visited Italy, my cousin Renzo pointed out to me that every family with the same surname, though not related, had a 'clan' name – much as one would find in South Africa amongst the Xhosa or Zulu. Our clan name is Cataena – which means, The Chain. Carla, totally innocent of this fact, would always tell me to 'break the chain.'

Throughout my life, since we met, I have borne her words in mind. I have consciously worked at breaking my family chain of abuse, negligence and rejection. My advice to my children and other youth has always been: 'Deflect ... Reflect.' Deflect the negatives and the shit that come your way. Deflect them with strength and purpose. Don't counter-punch. Life is not a martial art. Reflect the love you hold within.

Chapter
Four

When we settled on the name d'Offizi Pastabella for the restaurant Ian (my financial partner) and I were about to open, with my son Gianni as head chef and my daughter Gabriella as manager, I wrote to my cousin Renzo in Palestrina for the family's blessings.

He replied promptly and pointed out that our correct name was d'Uffizi and not d'Offizi. He said that the fact that I had d'Offizi on my birth certificate was a mistake of officialdom. Our name had been changed to d'Uffizi just after my father had left for Africa with Mussolini's army. One of our relatives was a catholic bishop who had impregnated an under-age girl. The family were so ashamed and embarrassed, even incensed, that they changed the name.

My entire family in Palestrina has the surname d'Uffizi.

Only my father, out of four brothers and a sister, retained the original name.

In honour of the family's wishes, the restaurant was called d'Uffizi Pastabella. Cousin Renzo arrived a few days before the opening to help with the preparations and to give us some extra Italian cooking lessons.

The family was proud that we were continuing a legacy almost as old as the hills of Palestrina.

I had sent Gianni to Palestrina a few weeks before the launch to learn from my aunts and other family members. My aunt, Zia Amadea, and her husband had owned and run a restaurant in Palestrina for nearly fifty years. Gabriella had been to Italy two years earlier where she went to Italian school in Rome and worked as a waitron in a village restaurant near Palestrina. Italian cooking differs in Italy not only from region to region, but even from village to village. Our cooking style would be that learnt in Palestrina.

The original deal was that my partner Ian would finance the venture completely, and the family would supply the 'intellectual capital,' as the working partners. On more than one occasion Ian asked me to sign collateral and I refused. His bank manager too asked me to stand collateral and I refused, on the grounds of our original agreement. However, a few days before the opening Ian approached me at the agency where I was working, told me he was in an awful rush and asked me to put my signature to a lengthy document he had with him. It was nothing important, he said, just part of the legalese.

I signed it.

I had signed collateral to the tune of R100 000.

It rained heavily the night of our opening and cousin Renzo remarked that in Italy an occasion rained-on was an occasion blessed. We were all extremely nervous about this new adventure.

The night after opening, we were fully booked. Gabriella and Gianni had screened quite a few applicants for positions as waitrons and I gave them both free reign to appoint at their discretion. The waitrons they appointed were all young, male and female, except for one, a woman in her mid-forties. She was not very attractive, overweight, but with loads of experience in Italian restaurants.

The restaurant was busy that second night and I was rolling home-made pasta when Ian came into the prep kitchen. He was white and shaking. At first he was incoherent and I was concerned.

'What's the problem?' I asked.

'How could you have employed that woman, she's fat and ugly? How could you?' he stammered.

My hands and arms were covered in flour. 'If you think I am going to employ people for their looks, so that you can fuck them because of your power as an owner, then I am going to wash my hands of this restaurant right now, so make up your mind.'

He was so angry about her he began to hyperventilate. A good friend of mine, Chris, who was helping at the bar, took Ian to the nearest clinic, where he was treated for his 'panic attack.'

He never forgave me for allowing her appointment. In time she proved to be one of the most reliable and popular waitrons we had working for us.

It's one thing cooking for family, friends and guests in one's home. It's quite another thing in a restaurant. Paying customers, and people in general, are extremely difficult. Almost daily the waitrons would complain to either Gabriella or me ... 'Table 1 wants the music softer' ... 'Table 7 wants the music louder' ... 'Table 13 wants us to change the music.'

It went on and on like a stuck record. One night a couple pulled into the parking lot and came to a screeching halt. They got out of their car, each banging a door shut, fighting with each other. 'Here comes shit,' I said to Gabriella. I was right. Nothing we did that night could please them. One elderly lady, dripping with expensive jewellery, complained about the paintings and prints on the wall, which were all from Palestrina. I told her as politely as I could that we were not running an art gallery. She insisted that she would never return unless we changed the artworks. 'Bye, bye, my dear,' I bade her farewell.

Ours was a labour of love. The work was labour-intensive, to our detriment.

There was not a single packet of pasta on our pantry shelves – everything was done by hand: cannelloni, lasagne, fettuccine, gnocchi, and linguine. We offered a selection of close to thirty different sauces: recipes from family in Palestrina as well as those created by Gianni, Gabriella and myself. We specialised in pasta and did not serve pizza. Our concept was traditional, simple homemade pastas. The only other meal served was steak, and that only because the demand from customers made it unavoidable.

We served a range of traditional starters like ricotta, parmesan and spinach gnocchi, and carciofi, artichokes lightly fried in lemon batter, which Zia Amadea had taught both Gianni and me during our visits to Palestrina. We also had an imported ice cream machine and I mastered the art of sorbet. We served lemon, orange, and berry sorbet and experimented with other fresh fruits. The sorbets were a hit. We also made home-made lemon liquor, Limoncello, taught to us by cousin Renzo. He made us promise never to divulge the recipe to anyone outside of the family. That too became a hit, and we served it to customers – free – after meals. A lot of people ordered bottles of the stuff.

After our first month's trading, fully booked every weekend night, Gabriella received a bill for over R11 000. At first she thought it was the rental. It wasn't. It was for the repayment of the capital loan from a local banking institute, The Good Hope Bank. Ian had financed the restaurant, but not out of his own money, as we had all thought. He had financed it via a loan.

I confronted him, and told him that had I known he was going to borrow the money I would not have consented in the first place. I could have mortgaged my own home to raise the capital.

The writing was on the wall. I had made a rushed decision to leave advertising and follow this dream. I was never any good at math, but I had no doubt we would need a miracle to survive.

In the meantime, we received rave reviews and had a lot of fun. One review from the doyen of Cape Town food critics, Owen Williams, was headlined: *'True Touch of Italia.'* Another read: *'Italian Gem in the Heart of Plumstead.' Cape Style,* comparing our gnocchi to four other well-known Italian restaurants in Cape Town and the Waterfront, wrote something along the lines of ' *... If you really want to taste good gnocchi take the time to drive to d'Uffizi's in Plumstead ...'*

Our regulars were very loyal. A couple arrived quite late one Saturday night after the kitchen had just closed, but we accommodated them. There was no more fresh pasta and so I made two special portions for them. Sometime later my daughter Gabriella beckoned to me. I was drinking beer at the bar. 'Come look at this, Dad.' I followed her into the dining section. The couple were sitting in their chairs, heads tilted back, sleeping. We let them be for almost an hour, and then gently woke them, telling them we needed to close. The next Saturday they arrived early, and my son Paul, who had also witnessed them fast asleep the Saturday before, greeted them at the door, asking, 'Sleeping or non-sleeping?' From then on they were called 'the sleepers' and when they'd phone to book they would simply say, 'Two for the sleepers.' They were regulars until the day d'Uffizi Pastabella closed its doors.

Under the weight of the loan repayments, the restaurant simply wasn't viable. Within six months I had to forego a salary. Paul resigned from the agency he worked at and he and I went back into advertising as a creative team. Gianni and Gabriella managed for another six months until the restaurant was sold.

It pained me to have failed. I consoled myself with the thought that – if and when I ever sit in a rocking chair one day – I will be able to reflect on my past and say, 'It may have failed, but at least I did it. And had loads of fun.'

Strangely, the most meaningful piece of advertising I have been involved in happened while I was working at d'Uffizi Pastabella. It was South Africa's Truth and Reconciliation campaign.

I had vowed that I would never return to advertising.

Paul, who was still working at the agency where I had previously worked, phoned me at the restaurant in a panic one afternoon. The agency was presenting the campaign to clients, including Bishop Tutu, the next day, and all they had was a logo design. No strap lines. No poster copy. Please could I help?

The budget was a miserly R1 000. Paul begged me to help. I refused at first.

I finally gave in, agreeing half-heartedly. I told him to come to my house to do the work. I also told him that my fee would include a six-pack of beer, to be delivered, ice-cold, with the brief. He arrived with beer and brief. We worked on the campaign for a few hours and, after a few beers, we had what we thought was a pretty good campaign. No clever, award-winning stuff; just a simple, solid campaign that would cross the diverse borders of the people it was aimed at.

When Paul and I normally worked on concepts together we would first look blankly at each other, searching the other's face for a starting point, an idea. Then we would get into the zone by discussing subjects like the universe, the origins of man, God – although, as Oscar Wilde would say: 'God is not a subject' – and even rugby, if we thought it could lead us to an idea. We dwelt a lot that day on human behaviour, diversity and quality of life. Quality of life in South Africa.

The campaign was successfully sold the next morning after Paul and his colleagues had spent all night putting it together. We had come up with the slogan: Truth. The Road to Reconciliation.

I wrote a poster that read: THE TRUTH HURTS, BUT SILENCE KILLS.

Paul wrote another poster: DON'T LET OUR NIGHTMARES BECOME OUR CHILDREN'S.

There were a few others that I don't remember now.

After hearing that the campaign was going ahead I felt I had done my job. But really my job was not yet over. In fact, it was only beginning.

The campaign started me thinking about the life I had buried. Things that were bothering me, and affecting me. Truths, in whose silence I had been complicit. I confided in my doctor and told him of some of my experiences. He said that it was my duty to speak out, not only for me, but for others. When I told him about Father Orsmond and Boys' Town, I became very emotional and confessed to him that I felt like a Judas for even mentioning it.

He banged both hands on his desk and said, 'Judas did not betray a guilty man.'

Chapter
Five

'WALTZING MATILDA, WALTZING MATILDA, YOU'LL COME A WALTZING MATILDA WITH ME, AND WE SANG AND WE SANG, AND WE ...'

Sister Maggie's voice rang out above the din and the chaos. 'STOP! STOP!' she screamed. Her face was ruby red and her hands shook. 'You are all out of key, out of tune, and most of you don't know your words, and Bart Nel, get over here beside me so I can keep an eye on you and your fooling around, now go stand with your face to the WALL!'

As Bart Nel passed her, sister Maggie gave his ear a twist and shoved him against the wall. She finished off with a tight slap to the back of his head. 'Now don't you move, Mr. Nel and don't you sing, not a fidget, not a word out of you.'

'Now class, let's start again, in tune and sing the right words, for the love of Mary!' Sister Maggie made a quick sign of the cross.

Sister Maggie was Australian, of Irish ancestry. She was born in Sydney and was fanatically Australian. We learnt 'Waltzing Matilda' before we learnt our own national anthem. We also learnt all about Australia and its history, and I knew where Sydney was, but hadn't heard of Durban. I knew more about kangaroos and koala bears than I did about our own bushveld and wildlife.

Of all the nuns in the home Sister Maggie was the kindest.

Sister Joseph, the Mother Superior, struck the fear of God into us. She taught arithmetic, which was my worst subject, and I was belted and cuffed by her more times than I want to remember.

Bart Nel was my best friend. We were the same age and shared our secrets – and any goodies we could lay our hands on – from time to time. I used to read his letters from home to him. They came maybe once or twice a year. He had difficulty reading, and he used to sit and look over my shoulder as I read aloud, following my fingers as I underlined each word, always asking for explanations of this and that.

I learnt to keep the bad news from him. There was a lot of it.

'Your dad's back on the bottle and he beat me the other night.'

'Your dad lost his job again. Your brother John is back in the "big house" for

51

assault.' It went on and on.

I used to lie to Bart and tell him that everything was fine at home.

I seldom saw my sisters, Lillian and Alba. Lillian was a class ahead of me, and Alba was still in the nursery section. No communication was allowed between the boys and the girls, so we rarely spoke or spent time together, except in classes. Of course, we always found ways of breaking the rules.

Going back is not easy. My memory for exact details fails me. I think we tend to forget a lot of the things that hurt us most. Of my eleven years in the home, there are only a few incidents that I remember – or want to remember.

I know for sure that I had my anger beaten out of me at Nazareth House. Like my father, I had a terrible temper, to the point where, when angered, taunted or hurt, I would react unthinkingly, and without care for the consequences. It was as if another person was operating within me.

The only team sport we played was soccer. I loved the game, and simply being part of the action. I especially loved playing goalie. One afternoon, two teams were picked for 'trials' to find the best players for our occasional games against other schools. Other than playing soccer, or idling about, or sword-fighting (using dustbin lids as shields and wooden swords, knocked together from planks or branches from trees) where and when blood would often be accidentally drawn, there was not much to do in our free time.

Behind the bottom goalpost was a row of almond trees and a high wall, one of four that made up the perimeter of this fortress. There was no grass on the soccer field. Lining the one side of the field was a row of small white-painted rocks, each averaging about five kilograms.

I was not picked for the trials. The selector of the teams, one of the older boys, and one of two brothers whose surname was Clarke, overlooked me despite the fact that I played quite well, was enthusiastic, and was, to my mind at least, a better goalie than most of the other boys.

The game began and I sat with friends on the sideline. I was angry. The selector, the Clarke brother himself, was playing wing and as he came running down the field, dribbling the ball, my anger welled up uncontrollably. I picked up one of the white-painted rocks, and as he was about to pass where I was sitting, I hurled the rock at him. It hit him square on the forehead and he dropped. There was blood all over. I panicked and raced towards the swimming pool, next to the soccer field, to hide. The pool was old-fashioned, with a one metre wall making up its perimeter. The rest was sunken. It was empty because it was cleaned and scrubbed during the winter months. The deep end was two metres, at most, and I went to the deepest corner and hid; naïvely thinking that I would not be found. Before long I heard Clarke swearing as he approached me. I crouched in the corner, holding my hands to my head. He gave me the hiding of my life. It was so vicious that, from that day on, I didn't lose my temper the way I used to. From that day on, I controlled myself.

Bullying was rife at the home. We learnt not to tell the nuns. Boys who did tell were assaulted at night, in their beds and fast asleep, by 'unknown' attackers.

Before the soccer season started the boys had to weed the field to prepare the surface. We (the smaller boys) would work in gangs under the supervision of the bigger boys. At this time the Clarke brothers were the biggest and the oldest.

One afternoon we were weeding. We would stand in a long row, about thirty of us, and in an almost rhythmical manner we had to bend forward, without bending our knees, and pull out the weeds in front of us. We had to stick to the single row format and move progressively forward in unison; like a little army of ants. If anyone straightened his back, one of the Clarke brothers would belt him on the back of the knees with a baseball bat. No straightening of the back, no sitting down to rest, no talking amongst ourselves.

An elderly black man worked at the home as a handyman and gardener, tending the chickens and turkeys. We heard that he had fought in North Africa during the war. His name was Ben. We called him Uncle Ben. He had often witnessed cases of bullying, but being a black man in those days, he knew his place. He was powerless. On this particular day, though, the Clarke brothers were mean and using their baseball bats with abandon.

Uncle Ben could take no more. Without saying a word he approached one of the Clarke brothers, wrenched the baseball bat from his hands and beat the brothers across their shoulders, backs and legs. There were frightened screams from some of the boys. A few cheered Uncle Ben on. Some of the boys ran in the direction of the dormitories, and soon two or three nuns came running towards us. The working party disbanded and we were ordered back to the dormitory block.

Uncle Ben was led away. A short while later a police van – we called them Black Marias – arrived and he was violently bundled into the back of the van. It was the late 1950s – to this day, I hate to think what fate awaited Uncle Ben. We never saw him again.

The thing I remember most was the constant drone of prayers, from morning to night. I cannot ever think of a nun without seeing in my mind a rosary. Mass was compulsory. Every. Single. Day. We would be woken at 5.00 am every morning; one of the sisters would put on the lights, clap her hands loudly, and call out: 'Up time ... up time!'

We would climb sleepily out of our beds, dress and wash our faces in the bathroom block adjoining the dormitory. We only wore shoes to Sunday mass and went barefoot the rest of the time; even in winter when it was very, very cold. We were given a change of clothes once a week, on Saturdays, and it was then that we bathed. There were two or three baths and the water was not changed during these bathing sessions. A nun would be there to scrub us down. There was a long passage, between the rows of beds, leading to the baths. Often, boys would line this passage on both sides wielding belts or wet towels, and we were forced to run the gauntlet to the baths.

Before going to bed at night, about 7.00 pm (in summer it was still light, and as we lay in bed we could hear the boys from Christian Brothers College playing on the fields across the road from us) we would say the rosary in a group, led by the Sister on duty.

One Sunday night a young visiting priest, who had played a little soccer earlier that day with the boys, chose a few of us to say the rosary with him on the wide balcony outside the dormitory. It was dark. We sat in a circle on chairs. After saying the rosary he chatted a little. For me, this was great – being up so late and having fun, talking and laughing. Then he started speaking about masturbation. I was no more than ten or eleven years old.

All I clearly remember is that he asked us to unzip our trousers, and together, masturbate. Sitting in a circle. He unzipped his fly first, and we slowly began to unzip ours; the young priest encouraging us in a gentle voice. Then we all masturbated together. I don't remember him touching or fondling any of the boys. Some of us ejaculated sooner than others. Afterwards, as if nothing at all had happened, he told us to take out our rosaries. We were going to say not one, but two rosaries, one after the other. As penance, he said. I will never forget this incident. It was hard to understand at the time, and still is today. Maybe the rosary ritual was an act of self-flagellation on the young priest's part. Maybe it had other meanings for him. Who knows. We just followed as a group.

There was another incident I will never forget. I believe that this one was the beginning of my obsession for women; and in a strange way, my love and respect for them.

I was very young and had only been in the home a short while. I was lying in a bed, cornered off by a partition, in the babies' (or very young children's) section of the dormitory block. There were only two beds, the rest were cots. This is how I know I was very young, no older than five or six. As one grew up in the home, you would progress from the nursery to the dormitory for bigger boys. The girls had their own dormitory. The other bed in this room, also partitioned off, housed the Sister-in-charge.

I was restless and in pain, tossing and turning and moving my head from left to right, constantly pressing my ears against my pillow; I had a very painful earache. I heard footsteps on the wooden floor, approaching my bed. A young woman holding a candle appeared from behind the partition. She placed the candle on the floor beside my bed and sat down next to me. In this bit of light I noticed – and will never forget – that she was wearing a pink nightgown. Her head was uncovered.

She sat beside me and wiped my brow with a face cloth. It was warm, and she spoke gently to me. This went on for a while. It was comforting to feel the warm cloth on me. Then she opened her gown and revealed her breasts. I saw that her nipples were pink. She took my hand and placed it on one of her breasts. Still wiping my forehead, she placed her other hand beneath the sheet and began to fondle my breast, stomach, thighs and penis. Then she took my hand from her breast and placed it between her legs, gently using my fingers to play with herself; moving them in and out.

I was terrified at first. But strangely I began to feel at ease; even curious and excited. A short while later she stood up, lifted the candle from the floor and walked away back to her bed.

I never knew who she was; she could have been a nun, or one of the bigger girls who often looked after the little ones.

It never happened again.

By contrast, when I was a few years older, a bigger boy, in charge of the pigeons, called to me and told me to come down to the field and help clean out the pigeon aviary. It was quite a big aviary, and we often caught pigeons in traps to keep there to 'home' and breed them. After cleaning the aviary, we sat down on two wooden crates. The boy lit a cigarette and warned me not to tell on him. He then opened his fly and told me to open mine, and that we would toss each other off. I resisted and said that I did not want to. He told me that he would give me a hiding if I did not.

By this time of course, my temper had been beaten out of me.

Many years later, when I was about 20 or 21, I wrote a handful of short, nostalgic poems about my childhood at Nazareth House.

I didn't mention my bad experiences in any of them.

This is one of the poems:

To have a pigeon cage and happiness
you need banana-crate walls
and wire mesh.
But, pigeons most of all!

The pigeons you must catch
in the gutters
of the clustered rooftops,
a pillow-case full at night,
when no one is around;
or set a makeshift trap.

We used to climb the rooftops
to catch
a glimpse
of the world outside;
sit all day long
trapping hopes and dreams
to fill
our cage.

Chapter
Six

Since my early teens, I have come eerily close to the presence of Herman Charles Bosman.

John McIntosh, my English teacher at Boys' Town, had stirred my interest in Bosman and his writings, although I had only read the few of his stories which were available. Only later was I exposed to his complete works.

Sitting in class, and often from my room in the dormitory on the second floor, I would look out over the fields, into the distance, toward the Magaliesberg Mountain Range, drifting beyond the mountains, in the direction of the Groot Marico, the farming area where Bosman lived, taught and wrote some of his most beautiful stories.

Just before my 30th birthday a lady who had read my poetry mentioned that she could arrange for me to meet Lionel Abrahams, one of South Africa's leading poets and writers. It transpired that Lionel Abrahams had been a student of Bosman's when he was young, studying creative writing under Bosman's mentorship. Lionel Abrahams was also the man who had, in recent years, had almost everything Bosman had ever written, published. Lionel Abrahams had invited me to spend an afternoon with him, when he would give me feedback on a collection of poems my lady friend had taken to him earlier. He spoke to me at length about Bosman. He liked my poetry too, he said, although he felt some of it was 'unformed and raconteurish,' but he gave me excellent guidance. He paid me a huge compliment when he told me at the end of our meeting that I should persist at all costs and that ... 'You are definitely a poet.'

It was only later that I learnt of Lionel Abraham's stature amongst the literati. I found him to be a humble man, and it was difficult conversing with him. He was wheelchair-bound, grotesquely crippled, and had a strong speech impediment. One moment during our meeting, the telephone, within his reach, rang and I watched him struggle, for what seemed an eternity, un-cradling the ear and mouthpiece. I was tempted to help, but somehow knew better. It was painful to watch. But he managed. I was grateful to him for taking the time – almost an entire afternoon – with me. I considered it an honour and a privilege. I still do.

Not even a year later a friend, Mike, and I took acid. LSD. It was my first-ever experience. Mike had taken it a few times before. We took the acid at his home in Kensington. I had been offered acid many times before, after leaving school and in the army, but, although I experimented with every known drug at the time, I was scared of the fact that, with acid, and depending on the state you're in when you take it, you have little control of yourself. Carla was with us, and she and Mike acted as 'guides,' which was (and is) essential for first-timers.

Mike, who traded in books, greeting cards and other stationery, lived near Bez Valley. Rhodes Park in Bez Valley is a large, sprawling area with lots of trees, picnic spots, ponds and water features. Quite late one Friday night, in Rhodes Park, Mike pointed to a row of houses opposite where we were sitting, and said to me: 'Did you know that Herman Charles Bosman lived in one of those houses? That's where he killed his stepbrother. Shot him dead.' I didn't know. I only knew that Bosman had been sentenced to death – the sentence was later commuted. I was now entranced with the thought that I had come so close to Bosman. The acid was starting to take effect.

For most of the evening I was tearing the bark from trees, and upturning big water lily leaves, looking for Herman Charles Bosman. The acid became very hectic later on, and I experienced a terrifying downer. I went to heaven and hell, and Carla and Mike both had their hands full, as I was to hear later.

The Sunday after, my friend Carey Fanourakis arrived at the door with a friend, George Howard, who was in his early seventies, and whom Carey had met and befriended at an old-age home in Rosettenville. Knowing of my love for Bosman, Carey had brought George along, because George had spent many years with Bosman. He was a retired journalist, and had worked with Bosman writing anti-establishment articles that the two of them published. He had also spent a few years living with Bosman and Bosman's then wife in London. He told me that Bosman and his wife had had a huge row one night – which turned into a screaming match – and his wife had said to him: 'Herman, you belong in the gutter!' To which Bosman replied: 'The gutter is the natural habitat of poets.'

Over the next few months George stayed over at our home during weekends, bringing me closer and closer to Bosman. George told me some incredible stories about the author, and told me that, before he died, his mission was to write his own biography of Bosman. There were quite a few biographies available at the time, but George insisted that a lot was based on hearsay, written by people who had never met Bosman.

After a while, George's visits became less frequent and we lost touch with one another.

Years later, I was about 36 and working in advertising as a copywriter for Bates Wells in Johannesburg. I was very friendly with a finish-artist who had his own office in the studio with us. One afternoon, after a late, boozy lunch, I went to pay him a visit, and found him putting the finishing touches to a portrait with his airbrush. On looking at the portrait, I went cold. 'I know that face!'

I said to the finish-artist, 'Is that George Howard? I know him!'

'Yes,' he said, and added, 'Sshhh ... my freelance.' When I enquired if he knew George, he said no, he had been commissioned to do an airbrush piece, based on a photograph of George, for a book about Herman Charles Bosman that would soon be released.

I immediately went back to the pub and wrote off the afternoon.

About five years later I was working for Bates Wells in Newlands, Cape Town, as a senior writer, and gave Alida Visser her first copywriting job. On her first day she brought me a thank-you present, nicely wrapped. Inside was a doorstopper of a book: *The Complete Works of Herman Charles Bosman*, edited, and with a foreword by Lionel Abrahams.

While working as branch manager at Swannees gents' clothing store in Wynberg, I would often sit at my desk and write poems, between my normal duties of managing staff and serving customers. One Friday evening, after five, I was entertaining a few clients, prospective clients and friends in the store. I had a budget from head office to entertain customers at least once a month, although there were always more friends than customers. I bought beer, brandy and good whiskies and served snacks and dips. There were always a few girls, too.

A very good customer, who spent a lot of money each month and was a nice guy, said he'd heard from our receptionist that I wrote poetry. He asked if he could borrow some poems to read over the weekend. On the following Monday morning, I arrived at the store to open up, and the same man was waiting for me. He said he wanted to have a cup of coffee with me and talk about my poems, which he liked very much.

'What the fuck are you doing working as a clothing salesman?' he asked as I was opening the doors.

'What else?' I replied, looking for the right three keys on the bunch.

'You should be a copywriter,' he said. 'You sell better and write better than any of the copywriters at the agency that does my advertising.' We entered the store. He explained that he was the marketing director of the Wool Board.

I thought copyright was a legal term. I had no idea that there was a career for people who could write and sell. I never read newspapers, only books. I never listened to the radio, only records and tapes. When I watched movies and saw those Brylcream ads, I thought they were made in America.

It had never occurred to me that I could in fact earn a living writing advertisements. My awareness did not extend to the media – life was a jol. Parties, women, friends, red wine and ganga. And, of course, wives and children. By now, I was married for the second time and had three children, two boys and a baby girl.

I was 26 years old.

Like all writers, I had always harboured the secret dream. Mario d'Offizi, famous poet. Respected short story writer. Being a novelist never really attracted me – I knew I didn't have the attention span to write more than a few thousand words. The dream had barely moved into consciousness, though, and now I was being challenged to pursue a career as a copywriter.

I thanked the customer profusely for his compliments and assured him that I would look into the possibilities. He promised to nag me until I did so. And then, things got in the way.

Like military service.

I wasn't really happy selling clothes – it simply paid the bills. I wasn't happily married either.

I heard from some of my mates that they were being called up for a military camp of indefinite length – unlike the compulsory one-month, once-a-year camps that dragged on for ten years. I was in the same regiment and had not received a call-up, so I got on the phone to my regiment and enquired why I was not being called up. Did they not need me? Had they overlooked my rank (private) and number? Whoever was on duty put me on hold, so he could investigate. He returned to our conversation.

'No,' he said to me in a flat, grumpy voice, 'you have not been called up because we don't know where you are. The Military Police and the South African Police have been looking for you for years.'

'But I informed the regiment of my change of address,' I protested.

There was silence at the end of the line. And then, 'Get the fuck to Wingfield by such-an-such-a-date.'

'Thank you,' I replied politely. 'Thank you,' I muttered again to myself. Freedom. Escape from an unhappy situation. I reported to the Wingfield base in two days.

I spent my final three months of military service in Walvis Bay. Since completing my military service seven years earlier I had completely lost interest in Southern African geo-politics. I had attended my first call-up, a one night induction into my regiment, situated in Newlands, near the famous rugby and cricket stadiums. I was berated by an officer who took exception to my long hair. My response was a quiet 'fuck you.' I never attended another camp or parade.

I disappeared.

I am sure if they had they really wanted to track me down, they could have. Cape Town wasn't, and still isn't, New York.

Now I started reading newspapers and listening to the radio. The papers were suggesting that South African troops were fighting alongside Jonas Savimbi's UNITA. The South African government was denying it. Everybody had an opinion.

The swiftness of our regiment's mobilisation – a day or two in Wingfield, a day or two in Bloemfontein and then a flight on an SAA Boeing to Windhoek, followed by an immediate flight on a cargo plane to Grootfontein – suggested that there was indeed a crisis. This was no usual one-month border stint. When we alighted in Grootfontein we noticed a few body bags lying on the tarmac.

We spent close to four months in Angola, fighting mosquitoes, flies and our own nerves.

While holding the fort at Pereira d'Eca and manning roadblocks on the outskirts of the town we would watch the returning columns of vehicles and armored cars. I saw one kid, no more than 18 years old, with a black moustache, deeply-tanned and with snow white hair.

When I spoke to one of his fellow soldiers, he told me that, over a period of a few days, their regiment had been constantly bombarded by Cuban artillery. After the first attack, the young guy went snow-white overnight.

I was shocked. We had only been in Angola for a few weeks. I shuddered at the thought of what awaited us.

The fear was constant, like a dirty shadow.

When we asked our superiors how long we would be there, the answer was always, 'Till this fucking war's over.'

Politics is the main weapon in any military arsenal – a fact we were unaware of at the time, and until long after. The politicians opted for a slow, calculated 'temporary withdrawal.' Our regiment made its way south, back home.

When we arrived home our regiment was given the freedom of the city. Our pipers leading the way, we marched to the Castle, a few blocks from Cape Town Station. Crowds lined the pavements. A passing-out ceremony was held on the parade grounds, within the walls of the Castle, and then we went home with wives, girlfriends, family.

Within two weeks of returning I told my boss where to shove his job, and told my second wife Margaret that I was unhappy, that I needed my freedom and that I was leaving. She could have everything we possessed. We did not own our own home. She could have all the furniture, pictures, bits and pieces, and could sell what she did not need or want.

I took my writing, notes and a few clothes. After communicating with Michael Guittard, my ex-geography teacher at Boys' Town, I took a train to Johannesburg and on to Magaliesberg, where he met me.

I stayed with him for a short while. By this time his partner, John McIntosh, had died. Mike was living alone, still in the charming thatched cottage on a smallholding adjoining Boys' Town, on the banks of the Magalies River. It was a place of temporary refuge. A place I could find my feet again and decide what the hell to do with my life.

Full circle. Back in the Magaliesberg.

I stayed with Michael for about a week before he introduced me to a couple who were living at the top-secret Nuclear Research Station, Pelindaba, near Brits. The husband was a nuclear scientist, his wife an ex-actress, managing a country hotel nearby. She organised a job for me as a barman and I lived in one of the guest cottages.

The letters from Margaret arrived at least twice a week. She asked for a reconciliation, to give our marriage another go.

Within four months, I was back on the train, having saved a little money, this time to Durban, where Margaret had moved with our little girl, Gabriella. Margaret originally came from Durban and her parents and brothers and sister were there. By now she had a nursing post at Addington Hospital on South Beach.

I moved into her flat, and soon landed a position as a branch manager for a clothing outfit – Cyril's Wardrobe.

Durban was a 24-hour holiday resort. I met up with old army friends. Women, marijuana and alcohol flowed. But I was restless.

Within a year, my younger brother Leandro completed his two-year military training and arrived on our doorstep. He wanted to go to Johannesburg to pursue his dream of becoming an actor. I wanted out of retail and clothes. Really, I wanted to try advertising. Durban was too small. I made enquiries at local ad agencies. The advice was 'Go to Joburg.'

Leandro and I decided to travel together. I had met a windowdresser at Cyril's who said he had a place for us to stay, any time we were in Johannesburg. 'Just give me a ring before you leave.'

The morning we left was one of the saddest moments of my life. Gabriella was just over two years old. When I hugged her goodbye, she clung to me, sobbing and screaming. She wouldn't let me go. Margaret had to tear her away from me.

I walked down the long passage to the lift without looking back. I've said goodbyes often in my life, but this – Gabriella's pain – will never leave me.

I left all my possessions with Margaret, once again, and took only a bag of clothes and my writing.

We arrived in Johannesburg the next morning and took a cab to Park Lane Mansions from the train station. My windowdresser friend, Doe Steyn, had arranged that we contact his friend Marion in Flat 32 – she would give us the key to his flat, Number 2, on the ground floor. The flat was empty, but it didn't matter. Marion invited us to have supper with her that night. In the meantime, she offered us a kettle, some coffee, sugar, milk and two cups. She also lent us a huge cushion – large enough to accommodate two, lying down – and some linen. I offered to buy ingredients and cook supper. She agreed.

We arrived at her flat early that afternoon to cook spaghetti Bolognese. Italian cooking was about all I was reasonably good at. She offered us wine, and we smoked quite a lot of marijuana. She had two young girlfriends with her, Carla and Mel. Carla was little and fairy-like, with big sparkling blue eyes. The biggest, sharpest blue eyes I'd ever seen. Mel was blonde. Carla was my choice, if there ever could be a choice, I thought.

After supper, Carla suggested we take a walk up the road to Hillbrow, for a drink. Leandro seemed to be hitting it off with Mel. Leandro was an exceptionally handsome young man. I often ask Carla why she chose me and not Leandro. She just had a feeling about me, she says.

We strolled up the road to Hillbrow, had a few drinks, and afterwards went to her brother Ray's flat, which she had been looking after. We talked into the night, and made love over and over again. I knew then and there that I would be with Carla for a long time to come. It was one of those moments when you know intuitively that all is right. All is good. All is meant to be. No analysis. No debate. No questions. Apart from two short separations, Carla and I have been together ever since.

Now, some twenty-nine years on, I look into Carla's brighter-than-blue eyes and in their depths and vibrancy I often catch a glimpse, a glance, of that other very special lady, Park Lane Mansions. And so we reminisce.

'Remember that time at Park Lane Mansions …'

Chapter
Seven

Those were some of the happiest days of my life.

When I arrived at Park Lane Mansions, my eyes were not yet dry from the tears I had shed at parting with my little girl. But, though feeling remorseful at my leaving – even guilty – I was filled with a quiet, confident feeling of adventure; new hope and new life. After two separations from Margaret I knew that our marriage would not work. I had seen so many parents wither away and their children suffer from a false, clichéd belief. 'We have to stay together for the sake of the children.' My thinking was completely the opposite. I thought, and still do, that we need to find ourselves – on our own if need be – for the sake of our own souls, our own personal growth. And, for the sake of our children, so that they don't become influenced by our unhappiness and frustrations.

I insisted on one thing only to Margaret. Don't let Gabriella get caught in the crossfire of our separation and divorce. We had made a solemn agreement to this effect and thankfully stuck to it throughout Gabriella's journey to adulthood. Her life today reflects balance and happiness, with a wonderful man and two beautiful children.

Park Lane Mansions represented a journey into the unknown. Not only did I meet Carla, I also rediscovered myself. I met new, inspiring people. I also saw a seedy side to life. Drugs and suicides. But with Carla at my side, as young as she was, I had no fear of the future. I knew that my life would progress, however slowly, to a level of achievement and happiness I had not known before.

Carla's belief and insistence that I would someday realise my dream of becoming a writer of sorts was contagious. It gave me back a little of the self-esteem I had lost since childhood. Her love for my children and quiet, unconditional acceptance of my two ex-wives also gave me a new faith in people. She often said to me, 'Mario, you have to break this chain of divorce with its messy consequences for the children. Your children will never, ever go into children's homes while we are together. Ever. You have to break this chain of pain and neglect and rejection. Think back to how you felt, and if there is any man in you, any compassion, any plain common sense, you will make it your business to break this chain.' And, she'd say on more than one occasion, 'Get rid of this Catholic guilt you've been dragging around with you. It's holding you back, dangerously.'

I had told her all about Nazareth House and about Father Orsmond. She was the first friend, lover and wife to know about the guilt that was haunting me. On occasion, for no reason at all, I would ask: 'Do you think I'm gay, deep down and I don't know it, or won't admit it?' She'd laugh, and say, 'But you're such a sensitive lover!' Chuckle. 'But be careful, love, because the boys do like you – and you're mine.'

Carla was just twenty-one years old, but she had convictions and a strength that far surpassed her years.

When Ray returned to his flat Carla moved into No 2 with Leandro and me.

Park Lane Mansions bred many legends. There was comfort and joy. There were tragedies. There was fun.

'Pipe Lane' (after dagga pipes), 'Mandrax Heights' (after those deadly sleeping tablets which are either crushed, mixed with dagga and smoked in glass bottle necks, or simply swallowed for a rave) cornered crazy Empire Road and peaceful Park Lane, which winds by the Brenthurst Clinic and up, curving past the Sunnyside Hotel to the Wilds.

In a sense, Park Lane Mansions was exactly like the Wilds, with the same extraordinary powers of light and darkness, stone and tree and openness. And seething with living things and vibrancy. The walls have since been felled, the rubble carted away. The rich roots have been dug out by the gravediggers of development. But Park Lane Mansions lives on in my heart and mind, and Carla's and my boys,' and in the hearts, souls and memories of many, dead and alive.

I cannot tell the whole Park Lane story from experience. My memories are of a mere fifteen months or so. But gathering the harvest of tales told by those before me, passed from mouth to mouth, I can sow in hearts and minds a small understanding of what there was. Of what has been destroyed.

Park Lane, with her majesty and her mystery, with her grand past, must have wondered about the types who filled her, taking shelter or refuge in her warm, once-sumptuous confines.

I doubt she ever turned her nose up at any of these. She was a real lady.

There were a few entrances to Park Lane, though only one was official. There were brown, sturdy, convent-type benches against high white walls, on a white tiled floor (the guy in No 34 used the decorated oak tenant name and number board for firewood one cold July night) and a cagey, gleaming brass Jack-the-Ripper lift. A broad, solid white marble staircase with wooden balustrades led the way up to the second floor. There was an elegant, gentle air of welcome.

There were quite a few exits too.

Had you lived or visited there you would have seen the Black Marias roaring into and out of the grounds from all directions, most nights of the week, filled with cops, black and white; some riding cowboy on the running boards, others jumping the iron fences bordering parts of the complex. The cops took away lots of folk who couldn't move fast enough ... drunks, prostitutes, the elderly; and the unfortunate innocents who just happened to pop in for a visit without their reference books.

Since time immemorial the cops had been trying to bust the shebeen at the bottom of the property in the old, dilapidated servants' quarters in the long grass at the waterway. From time to time, Park Lane also attracted other policemen ... plainclothes. But for different, quieter and more sinister reasons (one of which caused me to spend a long weekend in a crowded cell at John Vorster Square ... but that's a story all on its own. Many others who lived there at the time, and others whom I had only heard about, suffered a similar fate).

Don't get the wrong impression. Park Lane was a respectable place, really. The sweet old lady who lived in the flat next door to me – she called it an apartment – maintained two farms in the country. She remembered the tea parties, the Mayoral do's, the old stables, the first cars, the tennis courts, the elegance. She used to talk to me at length on the few occasions she invited me to tea in her apartment. She would talk about the old days, the care-free times, the refinements of a society long gone ... She could never leave, though. Because, she said, Park Lane had never lost, and would never lose, her elegance.

The caretaker in my Park Lane days epitomised in her character and her ways a creature of authority – helpless, yet still trying to put her stamp on everything and everybody. She was in total contrast to the tenants. She spoke broken English. She was fat, with a fatter daughter, whom she dragged by her arm to whichever apartment she went to collect outstanding rent, to complain, or to gossip. She complained constantly about this and that. Nobody took any notice of her. Nobody cared. She was difficult to understand, so it was best to ignore her, because, anyway, she never listened to our problems, never listened to our pleas, threats or demands for hot water, especially in winter.

We helped ourselves to the coal supplies – every apartment had a fireplace. Many a winter's night you heard the sounds of coal being hauled from its heap in the coalshed, and the stealthy scurrying of footsteps along the cracked concrete corridors.

My footsteps echoed prominently and happily along with the others on those nocturnal adventures. One afternoon, when my boys Paul and Gianni had arrived to stay with us, they made a little fire in the coalshed. It spread quickly, and soon the fire brigade arrived to douse the flames.

We never heard the end of it from the caretaker.

Park Lane accommodated a mixed bunch of tenants, young and old, couples and singles, lesbians and gays. And almost every tenant indulged in one drug or another.

Park Lane was where I met Jimmy-the-Greek. He was involved with the Greek mafia and arranged a job for me at a gay club in Hillbrow, The Together Bar, one block from Highpoint. I started as a barman. Then I stopped a brawl one night. It was late, nearing closing time, and two men, one a lot older than the other, lovers, stared each other down, squared up to each other. I reacted fast. Instinctively finding a little space for the palm of one hand, I hoisted myself across and over the bar and landed on my feet, inches away from them. 'Stop this crap,' I shouted and gently tapped each one on the cheek facing me, with a back hand. I was as surprised as they were. I was never a fighter, but had the ability to negotiate peaceful solutions. I had learnt this from so many, in so many situations. I also carried a small Beretta pistol, which my father had signed over to me.

They made me a bouncer after I stopped that fight. On duty I wore the Beretta visibly, tucked into my belt in front. After closing time one night, on my way home to Park Lane where Carla was waiting for me, I stopped at Fontana in Highpoint for a chicken-mayonnaise sandwich. I had forgotten to pocket the Beretta. I was in the queue when Alex (also Greek), the owner of a few nightclubs in Johannesburg, including The Together Bar where I was working, came walking past. He stopped, pressed a finger beneath my ribcage and said softly: 'Put that fucking gun away, are you crazy?'

The gun disappeared.

The work, and especially the hours, took their toll. And the girls, there were so many of them. So many single women and lesbian couples frequented the bar. The single girls, because there was no danger of straight men bothering them. When word got round that I liked women, the drinks came pouring in ... and from the men too. Some different, spunky and trendy women came into that bar while I worked there. One, in particular, had won a beauty (nude) title in Swaziland (no gambling, no porn in the South Africa of those days). She seduced me in her flat, a short walk away. She was my very first Blonde Barbie. But a street-wise Barbie, who later nearly had me beaten up when she invited me to have a threesome with her friend, also blonde and attractive. They had left the door of the flat open and the boyfriend walked in. The girls were half undressed, lying together on the carpet in the lounge. I had all my clothes on, and their love-making had just begun; the two of them kissing and undressing each other with a passion that aroused me enormously. I was sitting on the floor beside them, watching them, feeling their passion without yet touching. In fact, overcome by their sexuality, so uninhibited and free, just enjoying them enjoying each other so much and waiting for the signal to join in. Not that I had thought there would or should be any signal. It was just so different, this situation, so erotic and intriguing. Yes, I was horny as hell. I couldn't wait.

The boyfriend walked in, and when he saw the scene at his feet I knew that he had seen it many times before. But I don't think he liked Blonde Barbie, because he said something like: 'Not fucking you again ...' and told her to get out of his place, and take me with her. I'm glad I was fully-dressed. He looked at me menacingly. I shrugged my shoulders, and after swearing at me and threatening me, he let me be. He knew — and I knew that he knew — that I was just another sucker.

And so it went on. The recklessness. The abandon. The self-destruction. The uppers. The downers. The dope and the alcohol. The women. Not a moment of boredom. Carla, for some reason, hung in there. Patiently.

But I was missing my boys terribly. Paul and Gianni were with their mother in Cape Town. Carla knew this and offered to be there with me if I ever decided to take them back (I had been given custody after my divorce from Linda), even encouraging me to bring them up to stay with us. Carla was only 21, but already she had compassion beyond her years, and the maturity of a woman who had passed through more than one lifetime. I knew that with the sort of work I was doing it would be impossible. I was in contact with Linda and knew that she too was in a difficult position. She and her husband were separating and she had intimated to me that if I wanted the boys back, she would not stand in my way. She also intimated that, with her own insecurity at the time, she would welcome it, as hard as it would be for her to be separated from the boys.

I had to get a steady job.

I approached Cyril's Wardrobe – for whom I had worked in Durban – for a position at one of their stores in Johannesburg. Their head office was in Johannesburg with a few branches in the city, as well as two trendy stores in Hillbrow. I was re-employed as a salesman in the main Hillbrow branch.

Linda arrived by train with the boys a few weeks later, stayed a few days with Carla and me – they got on well together – and left. We enrolled the boys in a primary school and care centre. Paul was seven and Gianni just eighteen months younger. We also hired a nanny to look after them after school and to cook and clean. Her name was Sarah, and she was a disciplinarian. And a good cook.

My wandering days were over. It was time to concretise my life. Time to settle down. Time to calm down and be responsible.

Carla was now in full time employment as a draughtsman, and the rent and basics were taken care of. We still on occasion borrowed milk, coffee and sugar from neighbours. We drank once a week, when we would stroll up the road to the bottle store and buy a litre of our favourite red wine, Tassenberg. I took one too many days off work from Cyril's Wardrobe, through frustration and boredom, and one morning I was fired, without notice.

I deserved it.

Looking for something different, not wanting to go and work back in the clubs and bars of Hillbrow, I applied for a job as a salesman in Tony Factor's furniture store in the city centre. Somebody in the block had told me of a vacancy when I had mentioned that I had been fired.

The morning of my appointment, as I was getting ready, there was a knock on my door. The boys were at a school down the road and Carla was at work. A well-dressed man, about forty, carrying a briefcase, introduced himself as Bruce. He asked if he could come in because he needed to talk to me. He was a friend of Marion's, from upstairs, he said. I told him I had an interview and was running late.

'What sort of interview?' he asked.

I told him. 'What sort of money?' he asked again.

I told him — about R400 a month to start. He suggested that perhaps I should talk to him awhile. He had a better idea. It would be brief, and if I was interested then I would not need the interview at Tony Factor's. He was very polite, smiling all the while, and very determined. I was intrigued and agreed. I could always phone and cancel my appointment. Or say that I was running late.

Bruce was a friend of Marion and her boyfriend Theo, who lived on the third floor. Since welcoming Leandro and me to Park Lane and introducing me to Carla, Marion had become a special person in our lives. Bruce told me that he had read a collection of my poetry, which Theo had lent him, and that he and his wife Helen, who had taught English and Biology, loved my stuff. They were both breaking into marketing, planning to start a homegrown gift-wrap and greeting-card business, using indigenous South African artists. He told me how I could fit in and offered me R2 000 for the rights to my poetry. I did not even bother to cancel my appointment. R2 000 was five months' work at Tony Factor's. I was also to be a founder member of the company. Bruce had approached a few well-known South African artists and photographers and had secured their buy-in to his idea. They had also given him options on their work.

The company was called Paper Chain, and none of my poems was ever used.

I became Sales Manager and travelled to the major centres, selling our gift-wrap products to stationery stores and retail outlets like Dions and Garlicks. After two short years of static movement — we had reached a saturation point with sales, and had run out of funds — the company closed.

By this time Carla and I were living in a rented house in Norwood and the boys were settled in at school.

What next?

My interest in becoming a copywriter resurfaced and I began seriously to explore the possibilities. I contacted a headhunter in the industry and soon had my first interview at the biggest ad agency of the time, BBDO, in Braamfontein. The company was housed in offices on four or five floors of a tall building near the Civic Centre. With no experience, and based on my poetry and hands-on experience in retail management and sales, I was employed as a junior copywriter by the creative director, a superbly creative man, Rob Waldron who, the last time I heard of him, had his own ad agency, Waldron & Klatzko. He told me that I was one of over a dozen applicants — all with experience. But he 'just liked something' about me and my writing.

I started work within days of the appointment. And my life changed. I had just turned 31. Today, if you are in advertising at 31, you're already long in the tooth. But then it was an exciting, stimulating new world of experiences and possibilities and I was exposed to people and talent the likes of which I had never been in contact with before. Yes, I had met bright and talented people before. But never so many under one roof, working together. The dynamics were volcanic to me. I took to the pressure immediately and thrived on the drama, the intensity and the bullshit. I had also never encountered such arrogance in people before. I witnessed it almost every day, and was often subjected to it. It was a novelty to be exposed to people with such titanic, unashamedly cold and over-developed egos.

It took a week to gain a clear view of the smoke and mirrors of the advertising industry. On my first day I was invited by a senior copywriter, Sam Harris, and his art-director partner, Jules Joubert, for lunchtime drinks at the Saddle-Inn restaurant and pub, within staggering distance of our offices, as one of them had put it. The Saddle was a watering hole mostly frequented by the ad industry. There were quite a few other agencies in the area, so lunchtimes and cocktail hour were very busy.

I noticed that it was going on 2.30 pm and asked Sam if we should not be getting back to the office. 'Not a fuck,' he said. Jules said the same, and so did a few others with us. 'We'll get back in time for the pub to open at five,' said Sam.

And so, on my first day in advertising, I got pissed with my colleagues during a very late lunch and arrived back at the agency just after 5.00 pm, when we all went straight to the in-house pub. I was going to enjoy this new lifestyle.

Almost every day was the same. Warning after warning did not deter us. We'd be good boys for a day or two and then revert to our late, drunken-lunch habits. If the shit hit the fan when the deadlines and fuck-ups came, we would work late and weekends. We had a lot of fun.

I had never seen so many beautiful women in one place before, either. Advertising attracts the 'beautiful people,' I had always heard. Quite a few of the women were not there just for their brains or talent. One Friday night, sipping a beer in the agency pub (it was exceptionally busy this night), I looked around, a little melancholic and pensive, and casually counted six women with whom I had had sex in my short few weeks in advertising. I thought about this. Took stock of my behaviour, berated myself and rapped my knuckles, hard. 'No wonder they call you a dog ...' I thought to myself. 'How the fuck can you go so low?'

It wasn't as though I had done all the chasing. The girls were hot and naughty. After three months I was doing well – learning fast, coming up with a few good ideas, learning the ropes, writing easily in this new style. Then Sam and I were both fired.

We returned from the Saddle-Inn after 5.00 pm one Friday. There had been a crisis in the studio. A secretary had phoned the Saddle. The owner approached Sam, asking loudly, pretending to be seriously concerned: 'Is Sam here?' He was standing behind the bar, with Sam directly across from him, shaking his head. 'No, he's not here' the barman shouted above the din of the bar into the mouthpiece. He knew the drill.

The Managing Director fired us personally. He disliked Sam. He disliked his authority being undermined. Like everyone in advertising he knew that creative people were difficult, a necessary evil to be tolerated. He also knew that writers were hard to find; especially seasoned writers like Sam who had tremendous talent in his field, cars. But he had had enough. People told me I was caught in Sam's crossfire; that had the MD not had it in for Sam, I would never have been fired.

By then I knew the demand for writers, even junior writers like myself. I also had quite a substantial and reasonably good portfolio. By the following Wednesday I landed a pretty senior position at another ad agency – at almost double the salary. In those days, as in 2006, moving from agency to agency was common practice. Copywriters were always in demand, and if you were good, or even average, you could almost command your own salary. I didn't stop, moving from job to job, always moving for more money and a different environment, to stay stimulated.

The longest I ever stayed with an agency, Bates Wells, was seven years. Seven years was a lifetime in advertising. It was with Bates Wells that I and my art director, big Paul Metcalfe, after working together for about three years in Johannesburg, were transferred to the Cape Town office. When we were offered the transfer we were flown to Cape Town for a few days to conceptualise and execute a project. Paul and I agreed to the move immediately. It was the most painless and quickest decision I had ever made.

Chapter
Eight

Guy Murchie, in his book *The Seven Mysteries of Life*, writes that the ancient Chinese expressed 'the hypothesis of God' in their saying: 'If you keep a green bough in your heart, the singing bird will come.'

After the restaurant had closed, Paul and I marketed ourselves as a freelance creative team. We began attracting small clients and the time soon came for us to form a company. We chose the name Green Bough. Our logo was a bonsai tree. We were going to keep the company small, manageable and trim. We started off in a bedroom in my home and within months, after employing a designer, copywriter and a production assistant, we were forced to move to larger premises. We secured a little cottage in Kenilworth.

In the very early stages of our growth, when there were just the two of us, Paul treated me to lunch one afternoon. He thanked me, with tears in his eyes, for guiding him in his youth and for allowing him to become a 'renaissance man.' I was touched.

Not three months later Paul became a re-born Christian, and I the devil incarnate.

Life became hell for the rest of the family, because we would not change our ways. There was no way I was going to stop drinking beer or smoking. On a half dozen occasions I attended services with him. The church was a charismatic Christian movement, the services were held in a public theatre. I tried my best to find what I was missing. But the visits merely confirmed my belief in spirituality, rather than organised religion. I would not budge in my conviction.

And neither would Paul.

After a while we learnt to live with our differences – I more than he. And the Green Bough flourished. After landing the advertising for a prominent property group we moved into offices in one of our client's buildings in the centre of Cape Town.

We had a staff complement of six, although we hired freelancers when we needed to and at times had up to thirteen people working with us, including Gabriella, who did the books and all of the administration.

One day Paul said to me, 'Let's go big or go home.' I resisted a little, and then gave in. We called one of the top advertising recruitment agencies and gave them a brief to source a shit-hot managing director and strategist. Paul and I were sadly lacking in financial and overall strategic skills at the time.

A couple of candidates were put forward, but one impressed us with his enthusiasm. The new manager was in his early thirties and came with the required skills. We took him on and gave him total authority to take us to new heights. The potential for growth within our existing client list was excellent, and our new talent, we were quite certain, would take us places. I didn't count on him taking us to hell and back. But that's where we went.

After four years of moderate, and at times excellent, prosperity, The Green Bough went into liquidation. My bank manager conducted some discreet investigations and told me that the recruitment agency had not carried out due diligence on the new managing director.

It was too late.

My son Paul was employed soon after by a below-the-line agency in Cape Town that handled mostly liquor accounts. By this time he had turned his back on the Christian movement he had belonged to – after completing three years of bible studies – and was in search of fresh spiritual pastures. His problems with the church were both doctrinal and financial. He queried where his hard-earned tithes were going, and he and a few friends launched a mini-walkout. Quite a few youths followed.

I floundered a while and immersed myself, half willingly, into a deep depression. I was 51 and any hope of full-time employment in advertising had already faded. I sold my house, paid the bank, cashed in most of my insurance policies and braced myself.

Freelance writing was scarce.

My morale was rock-bottom.

My self-esteem non-existent.

One day Paul phoned me and told me that his agency had just fired their copywriter and that it may be a good idea to contact them. I knew a few of the directors and made an appointment to present my portfolio. Halfway through my interview the executive creative director, whom I knew casually from the industry, asked if I could help with some urgent radio spots the previous copywriter had failed to produce. The deadlines were extremely tight. I was shown a desk and proceeded to write the radio spots, which the client loved. By the end of that week I was offered a permanent position. Soon after, Paul became the deputy creative director.

Somebody once asked me how I could work under my son. I gave them the wise Chinese answer. 'If the student does not become as good, preferably better, than the Master, then the Master has done a bad job.'

Paul was better than I was. Especially in this area of experiential marketing.

I worked as copywriter with four art directors. Some days I worked with all four on different alcohol brands; supplying copy on tap. I have never worked so hard, writing so much on a daily basis, as I did then. I was sharpening my pencil, I told myself. The pace was so hectic, deadlines so tight, I was forced to learn how to use a computer – fast. I was scared of computers, and of my own ability to cope and learn new things. One of my young colleagues said to me, 'Modern technology is like a steamroller, my bro. If you're not on it, then you're on the tar. Where do you want to be?'

I chose the steamroller.

I quickly mastered the art and language of the SMS and wrote – or rather, configured – dozens of SMS campaigns. I had incredibly talented youngsters mentoring me.

We had a free bar at the agency, open every day of the week. We were allowed to consume all we wished. There was a joke amongst the staff that coming to work without a hangover was close to a fireable offence.

One day I was briefed to write the introductory copy for a phone-in promotion. It was for a major vodka brand, whose target market was middle- to old-aged black men in the lower economic groups. These consumers could phone a number, answer a question and stand to win 'some amazing prizes.' The main prize was a tidy amount of cash; the rest of the prizes were caps, T-shirts and other cheap gadgets. I wrote the copy: succinct and to the point.

The Client Service Director on the brand rejected the copy because it was too short. I argued that good copy should be short and to the point, especially if somebody was holding the phone and paying lots of money for the call to enter the promotion. I reminded him that the target market was largely made up of poor people. He replied that advertising was business, that the client and the phone service provider generated funds from these calls, and told me that if I had an ethical problem I shouldn't be doing this job. I reminded him that he had only been in the business for less than a year. I didn't bother to argue any further, but it confirmed what I always told people when they asked me how I survived the industry. 'I put my soul in my bottom right hand drawer and try to remember to take it home after work.'

The Executive Creative Director, who was also a part-owner of the agency, disliked me. He also disliked the young art director with whom I often worked. He disliked or had a problem with most of the staff. With me, the problem came to a head after he had briefed us on a print campaign for a baby and toddlers' milk powder brand. He rejected our concepts and ordered us to follow his direction – hyperbolic headlines and visuals demonstrating the efficacy of the product. I argued that any form of exaggeration regarding these kinds of quasi-medical brands would not be allowed by the Medical Council. Especially milk powders for babies and toddlers, those powders competing with mother's milk. 'Fuck them and do as I tell you,' he said.

We did.

The campaign went nowhere. The client rejected it outright. Life became more difficult by the day.

I was increasingly targeted, and only through the help of our Financial Director, who acted as head of Human Resources for the agency, and through the letter of the labour law itself, was I able to step lightly and keep my job. My daughter Mirella was still in junior school, and I needed to feed the family. It was during this trying period that I vowed to get fit, healthy and mentally strong. I did my best to keep a green bough in my heart.

My frustration caused me to turn to my own creative writing. One of my art directors alerted me to a Johannesburg-based web site, JHBLive, publishing homegrown South African writing. I submitted a few poems and a short story. The site featured me as Poet of the Month, and the story as Read of the Month.

I had written my first short story ten years previously, during working hours in an ad agency. I had just moved back to Cape Town in 1989 and was working in Newlands. Soon after my arrival a young secretary approached me and asked me if I could write a short story for her. A magazine was holding a love story competition and the prize was a trip for two abroad. At first I told her that I was a copywriter, not a short story writer, and that I wasn't interested. When she told me the entry criteria I was even less interested. It had to be a love story encompassing travel in an exotic location, boy meets girl. It had to end up happily ever after. I told her there was no way I could write a story like that, but that I would write her one, in my own way. Something that would probably not be suitable for entry into any competition.

I wrote throughout the day and completed my story by 5.00 am the next morning. It was about a ten-year-old boy and a-nine-year-old girl in a children's home who fell in love one night under a pepper tree. They would climb to the upper branches of the tree, where the boy would pretend that the tree was an airplane. He would get the girl to close her eyes and imagine. Making the sounds of an engine warming up, he would mesmerise her ... He would take her around the world, to exotic places like Bethlehem, where they witnessed the arrival of the young Jesus. The story had a happy, uplifting ending. A fellow copywriter typed it up for me and suggested I send it along to a magazine. I sent it to National Magazines and three weeks later I received a letter of acceptance and an offer to purchase the story – for R450. I was so shocked by this I did not attempt another short story for the next ten years.

At the encouragement of the editor of JHBLive, Andrew, I continued writing. The site continued to publish what I wrote. *The Cape Times Review* also published a story of mine in 2003. I also began an e-mail acquaintance with Andrew. One day he mailed me an article he had just written about marketing and colonisation. It was titled 'The New Colonial Game: King Leopold II, kiddie advertising and the colonisation of inner space.'

It was a riveting article and it made me feel uncomfortable doing what I was doing – helping to colonise the minds of people, mostly children. Through the article I also learnt some devastating facts about the history of the Congo – facts very different from the history taught to me at school. I didn't know it then, but four years later the Congo would change my life and ensure my final departure from advertising.

Meanwhile, I was stuck in the unhappiest ad agency I had ever worked for. Their staff turnover was frightening. To get fit and balanced I started power-walking a few times a week, and then began hiking with a group of friends I had recently met at my local pub. One Sunday, on our second hike together, our group walked up the Jeep Track – Constantia Neck – over the mountain, past the dams and back down.

Along the way I saw an old man who interested me. He had walking / hiking sticks in both hands. He must have been at least 85 years old. I said to my companions, 'This old guy, he's about 85 in the shade, and he didn't come up here by helicopter. He came up on his own and he is going back down on his own!'

Although the guys had already tagged me the 'senior citizen' on our first hike, I didn't consider 52 to be that old. The man we were watching was old!

I was to discover later that he would turn 92 the following year. He was small, thin, weather-beaten and dressed for the worst weather, although it was a warm day. That's age, I supposed. And experience, I was later to learn.

I couldn't get the sight and inspiration of that old man out of my mind.

The annual FNB / *Cape Times* Big Walk takes place in Cape Town every October. That year it was on Sunday the 13th. I toyed with the idea of giving it a go. Since I had started power walking, and with the image and inspiration of the old man on the mountain taking a firm hold in my mind, I decided to enter the 50 km walk. I didn't expect the walk to be a breeze. But I never guessed how I would suffer. If it hadn't been for the image of the old man on the mountain, still firm in my mind, I would never have achieved, or even attempted, this feat.

The race kicked off at 7.15 am at Kalk Bay Harbour. The inexperienced among the three hundred or so 50 km walkers sped enthusiastically ahead. I was one of them.

On the return stage from Simons Town, somewhere between Fish Hoek and St. James, I found myself staggering from side to side; my steps slurring, dragging me along. Sweat blinding me. The sun lotion mingled with the sweat and burned my eyes. I grabbed hold of the railing on the side of the pavement. I had slowed down to a pace slightly faster than standstill, a sort of wobbling, painful shuffle. My chest imploded. My head pounded. The beating sun didn't help. Even my nipples bled, chafing on the safety-pins attaching my race number to my vest.

Around this time, by now at least three hours into the race, I heard the voice of a walker, coming up from behind. As she came abreast of me she slowed down and said, 'You're in bad shape my friend, you should quit.'

'I'm going to Hartleyvale,' I just managed a mutter.

'You can't, in your condition.' I nodded as vigorously as I could, meaning I can and I will.

'Ok then, here ... share my energy bar and drink some of this.'

I did, and muttered my thanks. She picked up her pace, waved goodbye and powered on.

'A guardian angel,' I thought.

The energy bar and the orange juice gave me a boost that got me to the next water point, where enthusiastic first-aiders quickly surrounded me and iced me down. They also suggested I quit. I thanked them and continued.

The image of the old man toiling on top of the mountain was firmly entrenched in my mind. It was as if he were coaxing me along, beckoning me to follow in his footsteps. And at times, I must admit, my work anger also propelled me. I joked with my colleagues after the walk that it was the face of the creative director, appearing on the tar beneath my pounding feet, that drove me harder.

Seven hours, nine minutes and forty-seven seconds later – an eternity under the circumstances – having given my last and final thrust of energy and everything my mind could muster, I crossed the finish line, passing through a channel of cheering spectators.

A marshal congratulated me on my efforts and handed me a gold medal.

'What's this for?'

'You did very, very well.'

'Is this for my age category?'

She shook her head and placed the ribbon, with medal, around my neck.

'Can I smoke?' I asked her sheepishly.

'Are you crazy?'

I lit one anyway and painfully inched my way to the closest beer tent. My feet ached, every limb in my body cried out, my legs barely held me. But my mind was in a state of pure elation.

That Tuesday's Cape Times carried a special supplement with all the race results. To my astonishment I saw that I had been placed 74 out of 262 finishers in the 50 km walk. I silently thanked the old man. I was to thank him personally a few Sundays later.

As I had hoped, he was on the mountain. We were approaching the big pine tree by Woodhead dam when I saw him, off the path, a stick in each hand, slowly working his way through the fynbos and over some rocks. I broke from the group and headed in his direction. I did not want to alarm him by suddenly approaching him, so I moved cautiously toward him. I was a couple of metres away from him – his head was lowered, obviously focusing on the uneven surface of stones, shrub and rocks. I called out to him, quite softly.

'Hello!' He didn't hear me. 'Hello, hello,' I called again, a lot louder this time.

He tilted backwards. Sticks flew into the air. He fell on his back.

'I'm sorry, so sorry,' I said, bending down to help him up.

'Don't worry, it was just a little tumble,' he had a strong voice and a wide grin.

I gripped his hand and pulled him to his feet.

'I'm sorry to have done this to you but I just wanted to thank you.'

'For what?'

'For helping me through the Big Walk, in fact ...'

'Big Walk? I didn't do a thing.' And then, as if he knew what I was on about, he asked, 'How did you do?'

'I took a gold. I want to thank you. It was your example that made me enter. You were the inspiration.' And then, lost for words, overwhelmed, and a little embarrassed, I quickly said 'ciao' and moved on. I heard him call after me, 'Thank you young man, you're an inspiration!' I turned to wave and saw his smile as he gave me the thumbs up. I also heard singing birds. I composed an SMS to my daughters.

'I'm walking on clouds on top of the mountain.
If love's a spring, then life's a fountain.'

Chapter
Nine

I think that my lifelong love for percussion and the drums grew from the '... clikety-clack ... clikety-clack ...' rhythm of mainline trains, as I travelled home at least twice a year by train from Boys' Town, for the holidays. I travelled either to my home in Bloemfontein, where both my parents, though divorced since I was about ten, lived, separately, until I was about fourteen; or, in later years, to my mother in Cape Town or to my father on the South Coast of Natal. I travelled by train for most of my youth to and from schools and home, during my army days, and much, much later, into my forties and fifties. I have never learnt to drive.

'Clikety-clack ... clikety-clack ...' the sounds alternated between a low and a high pitch, making them not only mesmerising, but strangely melodious. It was like an incantation; but not as repetitive as a Latin Mass, and not nearly as monotonous. Nothing at all like the Kyrie, the dirge we choirboys used to sing at funerals when I was at Nazareth House in Kimberley, before I was transferred to Boys' Town. We choirboys and altar boys at Nazareth house used to do duty at the main cathedral in Kimberley from time to time, at baptisms, confirmations, weddings and funerals. We, the hired guns, usually performed these duties for complete strangers.

Nazareth House also served as an old-age home in those days, and so there were quite a few funerals in our own chapel. My nose will never lose the smell of incense. Nor will I ever lose the sight of open coffins displaying the faces of the dead, as I, with other boys, would stand at the head, foot, and sides of a coffin, 'swinging the smoke' as we called it.

The bells and smells. 'Clikety-clack ... clikety-clack ...'

I had just left Boy's Town – a little prematurely – and was on my way to begin my life.

I was 18 years old and Christmas of 1968 was a few weeks away. I would enjoy the holidays, after which, in early January, I planned to get a job as quickly as possible. I had the princely sum of R10 on me, and a little brown suitcase containing all my possessions. At home though, I had R40 in the safe-keeping of my mother. Some of that money I had by then already planned to use to spoil my mother and sisters – who were also living with her. And, with at least the other half of the money, I would open a clothing account and buy a suit, shirt, tie, underwear and socks, and new shoes for my first interview. My mother said that it was possible to open an account, as she would stand as guarantor for me at the store where she had operated one for a few years. This clothing store, in Main

Road, Wynberg, on the corner of Station Road and opposite Barclays Bank, was a family business, Rifkin & Miller. Their slogan, sign-written on the front doors and windows, and on a large sign above the front of the store, was, appropriately: From a needle to an anchor! You could buy almost anything there.

Earlier that year, while still at Boys' Town, I had won the R40 in a nationwide essay competition run by one of the few large, national departmental stores of the time, John Orr's. John McIntosh, my English teacher, received an invitation from John Orr's encouraging him to enter his pupils into their writing competition. The winning students would receive cash prizes, and so would their schools. The theme was: 'Ten Novel Ways to Attract Teenagers to Departmental Stores.'

I told John McIntosh that I'd love to have a go at it but that I'd never been into a departmental store. Back home, during holidays, I had walked past departmental stores, but I never had money and so did not bother even to go inside. He came up with an enterprising idea.

Michael Guittard, with whom he was living and who taught us Geography and coached rugby, suggested that on our way to play rugby in Johannesburg, before one of the up-coming fixtures – generally on Saturdays during the season – we could quickly stop outside John Orr's in the centre of the city, and I could run in and take a look around to get a feel of the store. I agreed enthusiastically.

One Saturday morning, on our way to play against Marist Brothers, Inanda, Michael Guittard kept his promise and parked the bus outside John Orr's. He said: 'You've got ten minutes, Dof,' and I ran inside. Those ten minutes or so were enough to give me a good idea of the concept. I wrote the essay. It was one of the ten winners. I won the R40 prize. R40! I was richer than I had ever been. I don't recall how much Boys' Town won. Father Orsmond wired the money to my mother when the school received it. Fortuitously, it was there to help me start my working career.

'Clikety-clack ... clikety-clack ...'

I was sitting in the bar-cum-lounge of the train, which adjoined the dining car. It was just after that evening's first dinner-sitting, about 7.30 pm. I was drinking my second beer, and, pen in hand, was scribbling in my black manuscript book, which contained all the poems I had written at Boys' Town. I was writing down thoughts about my experience the night before with Pamela, Father Orsmond's niece. I had been caught that night in Pamela's room by her grandmother, Ma

Orsmond, and had been promptly put on the first train home, after completing my very last final-year exam, Latin, earlier that morning. It was an expulsion of sorts. I was feeling melancholic and a little sad.

'Clikety-clack ... clikety-clack ...' I noticed a girl sitting alone a short distance away from me, closer to the bar. She was reading a book. But every now and then, when I looked in her direction, our eyes would catch. On one or two occasions, when I looked her way, she would smile at me. A quick, shy smile. I smiled shyly too. She had short brown hair, brown eyes and was waif-like and very pretty. Butterflies began to play havoc in my stomach, at first little tingles, and then, the more our eyes met, the more we exchanged smiles, an intense feeling. I felt waves of heat course through me, especially my cheeks. It was a delicious feeling.

It wasn't too long before a steward approached me, asked if I would like another beer, and whispered: 'The girl over there says you can join her if you'd like.'

Thoughts of Pamela faded as fast as the landscape moving by. 'Clikety-clack ... clikety-clack ...'

The butterflies fluttered faster as I stood up, grabbed my book, and, bottle and glass in hand walked awkwardly the short distance to the girl's table.

We introduced ourselves. She told me that she had been wondering what I was so busy writing down. Was I a student, she asked. I told her that I sometimes wrote poems. I did not tell her about Pamela. I told her I had just finished matric at Boys' Town and was going home to Cape Town to live with my mother, and that I planned to get a job as soon as I could. I told her that, apart from my love of writing, I had no idea what I wanted to do, but had already decided to follow the advice of a career councillor at Boys' Town and get a job in a bank. From there, I would decide.

She told me she was a final-year student at the University of Stellenbosch, studying philosophy and political science. She was Afrikaans, but spoke fluent English. Her name was Lizette. She told me she was twenty-four. She asked if she could read a few of my poems, which she did. She also asked if I would like to have a brandy and coke. She bought me another brandy and coke. Soon, we were drinking doubles.

When we were politely asked to vacate the lounge at closing time, she invited me to join her in her compartment. She was travelling alone in a coupé, which slept three, unlike the six-bunker I was sharing with a few other men. She also had some brandy and coke in her coupé, she said … we could go there and continue our conversation. I followed her along the narrow aisle.

A cold night wind was gusting through some of the open windows. We were passing through the Karoo. As the train hurtled on, and because the brandies were taking effect, from time to time I would cling to the rail on the passage side to keep my balance. She took my hand and drew me along with her to her coupé. Though a little pissed, I was nervous as hell.

We went in, she latched the door, and we sat down on the lower bunk. The middle bunk was folded up. Alone with me in the coupé, she was a bubble of laughter and fun. She poured us each a strong drink. We joked and talked excitedly.

'You can kiss me if you like,' she said suddenly. By now I was trembling. I kissed her. And again. And again. Until we were caught in a stormy embrace, hands fondling each other feverishly. She asked if I had ever slept with a woman before. No, I said with embarrassment.

'You're eighteen and you haven't slept with a girl before!' She sounded astounded.

I briefly remembered Pamela. I told her that I, well, sort of touched a girl most places, but, well … had never had intercourse.

'Would you like to?' She kissed me deeply. She was very kind. 'Don't worry,' she said, 'I'll show you how.'

She undressed and revealed a beautiful, toned body. Her breasts were smallish, pert and beautiful. Then she put out the lights and undressed me. Gently, while whispering kind words and instructions in my ear – nibbling my ear and neck from time to time – she guided me into her. I exploded very quickly.

'Clikety-clack … clickety-clack …'

We did it a few more times. She was incredibly understanding.

The next afternoon, Lizette got off the train at Paarl station, where she said her folks would be meeting her. We kissed, a little surreptitiously, I thought. When I offered to help carry her luggage, she declined and asked me not to come with her onto the station platform. We promised to stay in touch by letter and I gave her my mother's address.

When I arrived in Cape Town I wasted no time looking for a job. I used R10 of the prize money my mother had been keeping for me to open an account, put down a deposit and buy myself new clothes. I walked for hours, cold-canvassing, knocking on doors of the banks in and around the Southern Suburbs of Cape Town, where I lived. I was usually turned away, or told to phone for an interview. The manager of the Standard Bank on Plumstead Main Road, however, was very polite and encouraging and made a formal appointment for us to meet in early January the following year.

We met. I landed a job as a junior clerk, earning R90 a month. I hated arithmetic, particularly math, but decided that I would work extra hard and apply myself. I had not cut my hair since leaving Boys' Town, and from time to time the manager requested that I cut it. I always put it off with the excuse that I needed to wait for payday. Somehow, he let the matter be, or conveniently forgot to push it. All my friends had long hair. It was the sixties.

In the meantime, I kept in touch with Lizette. One day I received a letter from her, inviting me to spend a weekend with her in Stellenbosch. Not at her home, we could never do that, she wrote, but she could book us into a hotel and I could take a train there. She would treat me and pay for it all. She understood that I was still finding my feet, and how did I feel about the idea? I was ecstatic and replied, yes, yes, I would love to. On reading her letter I could hear her, smell her and feel her. I trembled all over.

'Clikety-clack ... clikety-clack ...' I was on a Friday afternoon train to Stellenbosch, hardly able to contain my excitement. It was early March, and I was trying to remember every detail about Lizette. She was there to meet me in her own car. We kissed and embraced, and she drove us to the Royal Hotel in the centre of the town. I was carrying a small overnight bag with a razor, toothbrush, deodorant, after-shave and a change of clothing. She had pre-booked the room – it was on the second or third floor, I don't remember exactly and after signing in, we dropped our luggage in the room and went back down to a cozy bar for drinks before dinner. She was bright and refreshing, with a playful sense of humour. She was as kind and gentle as on the train. She showed genuine interest in me, my job, and my dreams. She encouraged me to keep on writing and told me that she loved the poems to her that I had included in nearly all of my many letters. She really liked me. And I her.

I could not wait for dinner to be over, to be alone with her. Whereas I was only thinking it, she had the maturity – and the courage – to say it aloud to me. 'I can't wait to be alone with you,' she told me. 'I think I'm falling in love with you,' she added. I told her that I was feeling the same.

Back in her room she immediately jumped onto the double bed. Pirouetting like a ballerina, clasping her arms to her chest, she cried out loud: 'We have a whole weekend together ... two beautiful days, two beautiful nights alone ...'

And then she began to undress slowly. First her blouse, then her bra ... then suddenly she jumped from the bed and into my arms, her legs wrapped around my waist and hips, dangling above the floor as I held on to her tightly. We kissed feverishly, then she found her feet and, softly biting and kissing my neck on both sides, took off my shirt, unbuckled my jeans, pulled them down ... and we fell onto the bed and threw off our shoes and the rest of our clothes. This time she did not have to guide me. Well, not initially.

The lovemaking was exhilarating. She was not shy or as inhibited as I was, and encouraged me, talking gently to me from time to time, prompting me to explore her body as she did mine. Beneath me, astride me, with me also entering her from behind, as she had suggested, she coaxed me on and on to heights I had only dreamt of before.

And then there was a loud knocking at the front door, and, simultaneously, harsh pounding knocks on the glass veranda doors opposite.

'Oh my God!' she gasped, became frantic, and quickly put on the bedside lamp. I became limp. I iced up. I saw a terrified look on her face. She drew the sheet over her naked body. I panicked. I got up quickly and pulled on my jeans. The knocking became furious. I was confused. Which door to open first? I went to the front door, and unlocked it. An elderly policeman in full uniform barged into the room, knocking me aside, went straight to the veranda door and opened it, allowing another, much younger, policeman into the room. The younger man began swearing and throwing abuse at Lizette in Afrikaans, as she lay back, clutching the sheet up to her neck. She was trembling. The older policeman began swearing at me too, and I remember him distinctly calling me '... *donderse takhaar en 'n Kommunist.*' Literally, a damn long-haired communist.

He slapped and shoved me around a little. He told me in a quiet, menacing voice to wait outside the room. From behind the closed door I could hear the continuous swearing and abuse; Lizette sobbing aloud. Then the door opened and the two of them appeared, dragging Lizette, by now fully dressed, along with them. They both warned me, stopping to push me against the passage wall, shouting at me in tandem, that I was never, ever to think about contacting Lizette; and that I must never, ever put a foot in Stellenbosch again. I was to get out of town by first light the next morning.

Which I duly did. After a sleepless, fitful night; hurt and hurting even more for Lizette.

On my way out of the hotel I asked directions to Stellenbosch station from the receptionist on duty, a white, Afrikaans, middle-aged woman. She tried to avoid my eyes, but gave me the directions. She was not very friendly. When I asked if there was any money owing, she said that my 'companion' had pre-paid the bill. I enquired about the policemen who had come that night, and why. She said that the elderly policeman was Lizette's father, and station commander of the Stellenbosch police; the younger one was Lizette's brother. There was a slight smirk on her face.

'Clikety-clack ... clikety-clack ...'

Lizette had left me with a desperate longing, and an emptiness that would take quite a while to refill. I never heard from her or saw her again.

Chapter
Ten

We explained to Pastor Enoch that we were meant to be met by Bishop Lamba Lamba's people and were now very concerned. I could feel that he sensed every fibre of fear and uncertainty that we were feeling. He said not to worry, that the church had a branch in Kasumbalesa, helped us with our luggage and walked with us to the church – a ramshackle complex with a small church hall, pastor's office and an assortment of shacks and run-down brick buildings. A little pig was wallowing in a mud pit a few metres from the entrance.

The service was about to begin. We were greeted by the church's pastors. We gave them each a few French bible-books out of sheer gratitude for the refuge. They were genuinely delighted with the books. I thought if we ever get to Lubumbashe we may just be carrying an empty cardboard box.

The people were friendly, courteous and greeted us in French. I asked for water and we were served ice-cold bottled water on a tray. We slumped wearily into the plastic chairs at the back of the church hall, sighed, and smiled nervously at each other.

It was a temporary relief.

We composed ourselves, quietened our nerves and emotions for a brief moment, and got to work. Matt set up the tripod with his camera and I started taking random footage of pastors – all neatly dressed in suits and ties. Footage of men, women and children in the congregation. Anything to keep myself occupied.

There was a band on stage with drums and electric guitars, just like the charismatic churches I had attended in Cape Town. I was surprised, however, to see so few people attend this Sunday service. Matt reminded me that the place was a whorehouse and a smugglers' den, after all.

The service began with a warm-up from the band. Then two pastors started preaching, one in French, the other repeating the words in Swahili.

Meanwhile, Pastor Enoch had arranged transport to Lubumbashi. Halfway through the service we were told to pack up our gear, and were escorted into the presence of the Office Pastor. We gathered in his little office where he prayed for our safe journey. The Office Pastor's son was sent to accompany us, and to ensure our safe arrival in Lubumbashe.

The road to Lubumbashe is narrow, with no white lines in the middle, and just wide enough for a truck and car to pass each other. Looking forward, the road appeared like a thick slab of tar stuck to the earth, with a drop of about a half a metre on either side. The landscape was ominous. Dark, dense bush – unvarying in texture, colour and thickness – passed us by, kilometre after kilometre.

Every here and there we would pass a small clearing with thatched mud huts, where the locals would be selling bags of charcoal, maize, sweet potatoes and the strangest looking tomatoes I had ever seen – they looked like wrinkled yams, or a strange cross between tomatoes and sweet potatoes. Some were dusty red, some tinged with orange, some an ochre-yellowish colour. No two were the same shape. They looked nothing like the round, almost identical supermarket reds that I was used to.

We stopped on two occasions, when Pastor Enoch bought bags of maize, potatoes and tomatoes. He had to remove some of our luggage from the boot to accommodate his wares. For the rest of the journey the luggage weighed heavily on our laps. I was about to ask him to stop so I could bury the crystal Steve Minaar had given me back in Cape Town, when a little voice suggested I hold on to it for a while.

We also stopped at a few military roadblocks on the way. Three, four? I wasn't counting.

When I saw the first, my heart began to race and my mouth dried up with fear. The next few induced the same feelings. On each occasion the driver would climb out of the car, approach the soldiers, who were armed with a variety of weapons, some bearing more than one, sign a piece of official-looking paper, pay a toll or bribe and we would move on.

It was 120 km to Lubumbashe.

As we neared the city, the first thing I noticed was a huge mining complex that stood on the outskirts like a colossus. By this stage the tar road had ended and we bumped along a pot-holed dirt road that wove through a maze of outer suburbs of the city. We sat patiently in the back of the car. After my experience at the border, I was struggling to stifle that terrible fear of the unknown and resign myself to fate.

Whatever it may be.

We drove around for what seemed an eternity, and then stopped outside a run-down group of houses, Pastor Enoch's place. We helped him unload his goods.

He briefly introduced us to his wife and father-in-law and then we set off through the maze of rough roads, down-trodden houses and the odd shack. Unlike the cities of South Africa, there were very few shacks about.

When we arrived at the Come and See Church, we entered the little driveway and parked. We unloaded our bags and were led into the church hall, where we laid our luggage on the floor and were shown to a wooden bench. Everything we heard was either in French or Swahili, but mostly French. Pastor Enoch tried to make us feel as welcome as he could, told us not to worry, and that he would look after all arrangements.

About an hour later, we were confused and uncertain, not knowing what was happening, when a tallish, slimly-built man approached us with the bearing of a military officer – but in a splendid suit and tie. He introduced himself in English as Pastor Jeff and abruptly and unsmilingly informed us that he was the Office Pastor and the man who received all visitors to the church. He used the word protocol a few times. He pulled up a white plastic chair and sat down facing the pair of us.

'We have a problem.' Just like that. Once again, my heart sank. The roller-coaster plunged. I glanced at Matt and saw amazement on his face. And then anger, reddening his cheeks. Mine had paled, even whitened, by then. Matt became adamant. 'But all the arrangements were made through Pastor Oscar in Johannesburg, there were emails informing you of our trip ... we have come to make a documentary ...'

Pastor Jeff cut him off in mid-sentence, looking at Matt coldly. 'We have a problem. I saw emails, but there was no specific time, and I am preparing for a trip to Cape Town. I was not informed.' I jumped into the debate and almost in unison, Matt and I insisted that we had been with Pastor John, from Zambia, the previous day and had heard him on his cell phone to Bishop Lamba Lamba, telling the bishop that we would be at the border when it opened at 8.00 am. Pastor Jeff ignored this and told us that we would have to wait for the bishop, who was in a meeting. He stood up abruptly and informed us that he would arrange refreshments.

Pastor Enoch followed him out of the door, talking excitedly in French and waving his arms in the air. Meanwhile, we were offered a drink, Fanta or Coke, by a courteous young lady.

When Pastor Enoch returned a short while later I asked him what was going on.

He explained the situation. 'Pastor Jeff is being very difficult. And I have told Pastor Jeff that, even if you were heathens and had no business with the church, you should be shown Christian compassion and given safe refuge.' Pastor Enoch was agitated, and concerned.

We did not know that the transport to Lubumbashe was a taxi. The driver, now caught in the middle of this conflict, was waiting for his money, and getting angrier by the minute. We only had R700 on us – meant to pay our way back to Lusaka.

Matt became really angry and told me that if they did not sort things out we'd go back to Zambia.

'How are we going to do that, Matt?'

'Walk. If we have to.'

Then things changed very quickly. Pastor Jeff returned, sat in the white plastic chair and shifted about uncomfortably. He ground his teeth. His cheeks seemed to swell as he did so. 'Welcome to the DRC. In a few moments we will meet the bishop and then we will eat.'

The roller-coaster reached upward.

The taxi driver was paid.

Pastor Enoch bade us farewell. Matt and I both hugged and thanked him. For the first time in a long time we breathed easily.

The bishop was a short, portly man with a gentle, open face. He welcomed us to the DRC in broken English, thanked us for coming, and wished us well during our stay. Food was served on a long table in the hall. Pastor Jeff introduced us to the eating customs of the Congo. We washed our hands in a big blue metal bowl of water, took a plate and helped ourselves from a selection of fatty pork knuckles, sadsa, little pieces of river fish – called Rouge – and Chinese cabbage. It was delicious, especially the fish. After eating, we washed our hands in the same bowl of water, this time with a little liquid soap added. Almost immediately Pastor Jeff said to collect our luggage and follow him. He had just come out of the bishop's office. He was also carrying a large pile of Congolese francs. They were brand new notes, neatly wrapped in plastic.

Parked outside was a dark green Toyota with RTIV Presse sign-written on the side doors and on the back of the car. Pastor Jeff explained that the church had their own radio and TV station, which was screened 24 hours a day in the Congo. We climbed into the car and the official driver took us not too far from the church, to what appeared to be the centre of Lubumbashe.

We parked outside the Hotel Babel. I thought immediately about the Tower of Babel.

As we were busy unloading our luggage we both noticed a youngish white man in shorts and hiking boots standing smoking beside a car, a few metres from the hotel entrance. Matt and I glanced at each other in amazement.

Pastor Jeff led us into the hotel foyer where we were greeted by a policeman in a blue uniform, with a 9 mm Uzi machine gun slung over his shoulders. Pastor Jeff spoke briefly to the concierge, took a key hanging on a wooden rack behind the front desk — as if he knew the place inside out — and led us up a stairway, then left down a dingy corridor, to room No 6.

Walking down the corridor, he sniffed in disgust at the smell of stale tobacco. His voice filled with authority. 'As Christians you do not smoke or drink. And no women.' It was a command. If only he knew how desperate we were for a cigarette (the only other person I know who smokes as much as I do is Matt; we made a fine pair!) and a beer.

Pastor Jeff opened the door of our room. 'Welcome, here is your room, put your bags down while I pay downstairs.' And the roller-coaster plunged.

It was a small room with one three-quarter bed, no basin, no carpets, no furniture; just a rickety, dirty white table and a coat rack. A blue curtain hung sloppily from the wall to the right of the bed. I drew it open, hoping for a view. There was a closed window-frame, and behind it, a concrete wall. There was another hole in the wall on the left side of the bed. It had jail-type bars, and behind these, a geyser.

Pastor Jeff returned a short while later. 'Bring your cameras and equipment and let's go.'

We went back to the church to film the evening service.

As we entered the church the service was about to begin. I looked in awe at the packed congregation seated on plastic chairs and benches. There must have been close on three thousand people. It was dark, and only the stage was lit. On a table on the stage there were vases full of plastic roses, lilies and other flowers. The bandsmen were tuning their instruments. People were praying, babbling in tongues and weeping; a few lay prostrate in the aisles.

The bishop stood on the stage with another pastor and the service began, led by the bishop in French, while the other pastor repeated his words in Swahili. Pastor Jeff gave us the freedom to film anywhere, anything, so long as it was inside the church only. Nobody outside must know we have cameras, he instructed. Matt had the camera mounted on the tripod for master shots. I roamed through the aisles, shooting at random.

There was an incredibly powerful energy in the place. I flowed with it, focusing on what I was doing. At times, looking through the viewfinder, I was mesmerised by the crowds. Then Pastor Jeff brought Matt and me together at one of the entrances and explained that we would be going on stage to be introduced to the congregation by the bishop himself. Now I knew why he had asked us earlier for our full names, which he had written down on a piece of paper.

Pastor Jeff led us onto the stage and we were introduced to the congregation by the bishop, who shook our hands in turn. Neither of us could speak French, but we noted the words Journaliste and Afrique de Sud. We were applauded.

The service continued. The fervour of the congregation, the preachers and the band reached a crescendo. To me, it bordered on mayhem. I continued to film as calmly as I could. After a while the noise and the heat became unbearable. I stepped outside, placed my camera in the side pocket of my photographer's jacket and stood and stared across the road, into the darkness.

I felt a terrible sense of déjà vu.

My body went cold. I turned my head and saw Matt approaching.

I told him what had happened.

Strange, he said, he himself had earlier felt a similar feeling. And then Matt said an eerie thing.

'Maybe your mother and great-grandmother lived in one of those houses across the road.'

My body iced-up. I had forgotten what I had told Matt, sometime ago, before we left home. Back in Cape Town, when Matt first invited me to the Congo, I looked up an old atlas I had at home and did a little research to familiarise myself with the region. When I saw the names Katanga and Elizabethville, my childhood flooded in.

* * *

When I was growing up, my mother often spoke to me about her own childhood. How she grew up happily with her grandparents, until she was eight or nine years old, in a charming little town called Elizabethville, in the Katanga province of the Belgian Congo. When I asked why she lived with her grandparents and not her parents she explained that her mother died while giving birth to her. And her father had drowned when her mother was just six months' pregnant. She never saw her parents. Not once. Her grandmother was a missionary and an ex-singer and dancer. Her grandfather was a wayward, red-bearded, red-haired Irishman. He captained a cargo boat on one of the many rivers in the region. She wasn't sure which one. Her grandfather was a heavy drinker. For weeks at a time she would accompany him on the cargo boat.

Up and down the river, she said.

He often got her up on the bar counter and made her dance and sing 'Knees up Mother Brown' to entertain the crew and passengers.

One night, he rested his head on his arms on the bar counter and died right there.

'It must have been the whisky,' my mother said.

That was when she was about six years old. Two or three years later, her grandmother died of Blackwater fever. She was sent to the Langlaagte orphanage, south of Johannesburg. After the Belgian Congo gained its independence in 1960, Elizabethville was renamed Lubumbashe

My mother led a colourful, but tough and tragic life.

When we discovered that we were only half sister and brother, Lillian and I were very sad and we sobbed for a while, holding each other. But we also comforted ourselves and reminded each other that we at least had the same mother and were still brother and sister, no matter what.

Alba and Leandro were my full siblings.

My mother had been married before and had five children, four boys and a girl. David, her first-born, then Wally, Eileen, Monty and Victor, in that order. When my mother met my father she was already a few months pregnant with Lillian. At this time, David, Wally and Eileen were living with their paternal grandparents in Cape Town. Victor and Monty were in children's homes.

Their father's name was David Hemmings. His friends called him Sonny. My mother referred to him, scornfully, as Hemmings. She used to tell me how he frequently beat her up. And how violently jealous he was.

She told me of the time he took an axe to her and she had to run for her life. The neighbours, she said, called the cops who simply gave him yet another warning. The beatings didn't stop while they were together. His jealousy knew no bounds, and he frequently accused her of having secret affairs with his own friends, she said.

When they gathered in his home to drink and play cards, she was not allowed any contact with his friends. She had to stay in the kitchen and wait for him to bark orders.

'Joyce, shut the kids up!'

'Joyce, bitch, fetch more bloody drinks!'

'Make more food, bring more bread, and clean these fucking ashtrays ...!'

My mother was a very beautiful woman. It was only much, much later that I learnt she had an eye for the men and would flirt at any given opportunity. David Hemmings would make her meet him after work at his local. When she arrived at the pub, with the three elder kids in tow, and the younger two in a pram, she would have to wait outside until he was ready, no matter what the time or the weather. And, if he was not ready to leave when she arrived, she would simply have to wait.

'God help me if I didn't,' she said. 'Come rain or bladdy South Easter, the bastard would make me wait for him, and sometimes the kids, especially the little ones in the pram, would yell their heads off.'

It was because of David Hemmimg's asthma, and serious tuberculosis, that the doctors in Cape Town suggested he move to a crisper, dryer climate for at least a few years to get better. He and my mother – without their children – arrived in Bloemfontein in 1948, where she met my father.

My father was a master builder and stonemason and had just been released as a prisoner of war. He had been part of a group of Italian prisoners who had been placed in the protective care of local farmers, as general labourers. David Hemmings had made enquiries for a good, cheap Italian prisoner, a skilled artisan to renovate his home.

My father had been recommended, and that's how my parents met. It wasn't long before my mother and he began an affair.

One day, while building an outside wall, my father heard screams from inside the house. David Hemmings was cursing drunkenly at the top of his voice. 'You fucking bitch, you've been messing around with that fucking eyetie ... don't lie to me!' My father knew instinctively what was happening and, in a blind rage, stormed into the house, and beat up David Hemmings.

'Your father dragged Hemmings out of the house, lifted him up and threw him over the wall he was building and Hemmings landed there on his arse for the neighbours to see,' my mother told me, with a sly smirk on her face.

My father was also an extremely jealous man, with a volatile temper. He was also much more powerful than the sickly David Hemmings. Not too long after that incident my father and mother moved in together – into a room in a boarding house.

David Hemmings returned to Cape Town.

I only met him in Cape Town when I was fourteen, and by then he was a pastor in the Church of England, serving amongst the poor. He took me on as a son. I did not stay with him, but went for the occasional Sunday lunch when my mother was broke, and gardened for him for tea and cake and pocket money. I liked him very much and inwardly apologised for all the pain my mother and father had put him through. But he did not need apologies, or sympathy. He had turned into a strong, powerful and resilient man who deeply cared about others.

This was also where and when I met my half-brothers, Victor and Monty, for the first time. I had met David, Wally and Eileen on a few occasions while I was growing up. David was an actor, who played many a role in Shakespearian plays staged at the open-air theatre in Wynberg, Cape Town, and was a Western Province body-building champion.

In his early twenties – he is 14 years older than me – he wrote a play, *Iron Bars*, which protested the apartheid regime. He was living and working in Port Elizabeth at the time. On the first night of the play, during interval, security police swarmed backstage and closed the show down. Banned. David was detained for a while. On his release he left South Africa, spent some time in Rhodesia, then headed off to Spain, and then on to Canada, where he became a citizen.

Wally was my favourite brother. Whenever he visited my mother in Bloemfontein, he used to ride the 100 km to Kimberley on his scooter to spend the day with us at Nazareth House. He was a printer, working for the *Cape Argus* daily newspaper in Cape Town.

Eileen, on her occasional visits from Cape Town, when we were home on holiday, would cuddle us, spoil us and buy us all sorts of treats.

I remember my mom telling me that Monty was named after a famous general from the Second World War. When I did eventually meet him he was a policeman. And Victor was a male nurse.

I remember being very impressed by their uniforms.

* * *

When the service finally ended, Pastor Jeff again commanded 'Let's go.'

He dropped us at the hotel and said he would see us about nine the next day. The policeman with the Uzzi asked us for money. We pleaded poverty. We were both craving a cigarette. We went upstairs to the room, battled to open the faulty lock, entered, dropped our gear and sat at the edge of the bed. We looked at each other in silence.

We agreed not to smoke in the room just in case Pastor Jeff surprised us. We stepped out of the door and stood in the little toilet right next to our room, smoked, and, through the metal bars, looked down into the street. We smoked about three cigarettes each, one after the other. Back in the room, we sprawled on the bed and shared thoughts and feelings.

I knew the risks I had taken coming to this place. There was no time for regrets.

Besides, I was secretly enjoying the adrenalin rush. Although we were pissed off at the treatment we had received, we laughed and joked. Welcome to the DRC! The Congo! Welcome to hell!

I then formally renamed Pastor Jeff Joseph Goebbels.

We were exhausted. Hungry. But happy we had got this far. We were preparing for bed when we heard footsteps in the passage approaching us. It was about 10.00 pm. Danger? The roller coaster started its plunge downwards, when suddenly a loud voice cursed. *'Die donderse, fokken bliksems!'* Matt and I looked at each other in utter amazement. A South African. More than that, an Afrikaaner! We heard the door right next to ours open. We jumped up, Matt leading the way, and barged into the room. There, with a black woman, was the white man we had seen earlier in front of the hotel.

They were just as surprised as we were.

In our excitement and jubilation, we introduced ourselves. His name was Danny and she was Rauha. They were from Windhoek in Namibia. They invited us to sit on the floor and we smoked and talked into the early hours of the morning.

Their story is a book on its own. They were in the Congo on 'business.' They had been here three months earlier and had needed to leave in a hurry. They had left a brand new car with some Congolese connections and $3 500 dollars in the bank. When they returned, just a few days before we arrived, they found their car had been used as a taxi, with 80 000 km on the clock. It was badly damaged. And their bank account was completely empty.

Rauha, an Ovambo from Namibia, described the locals as primitive. I won't use her exact words.

We left their room at about two in the morning, locked our door, placed the table by the door – trusting nobody – and tried to sleep. I mentioned to Matt that we had just met another pair of angels. A most unlikely pair, I added. He agreed. Over the next two days Danny and Rauha became comforting friends. And a mine of information: What to do. What not to do. Whom to be wary of.

The bed crawled with lice. The ground forces, we called them. The mosquitoes attacked from the air. Every so often we would get up, switch the light on and splatter any mosquitoes we found clinging to the walls. I killed one on the wall above our bed. We were amazed at the amount of blood on my palm and on the wall. Matt grabbed his camera and took a photo. One for the scrapbook, he said. Restless, we went back to the toilet. Had a smoke. Back to bed. Lights out.

Stretched out on our backs in the dark, we rewound the day, every moment we could recall, opened up the pressure valves and literally cried ourselves to sleep with laughter. We awoke at about 6.00 am, after less than three hours' sleep.

We had a few cigarettes in the toilet. Then back to the room. Read a little. Talked a little. More cigarettes. No worries, Goebbels will collect us at nine. Matt reminded me not to hold my breath. Goebbels would most certainly be a few hours late. We decided to take a stroll. Wherever we went people begged for money. There were armed soldiers and police everywhere. Danny knew the place and told us that the police, soldiers and traffic police were all military.

They just wore different uniforms. The soldiers were clad in olive-green battledress. The police wore blue uniforms and the traffic police were dressed in blue trousers, bright yellow shirts and yellow helmets. The immigration officers – the Gestapo – wore black pants and white shirts. On each shoulder of their shirts was a black epaulette with a single white star embroidered on it.

Everywhere, on every street we walked, there were money-changers. They would sit beside their little tables piled with money, mostly Congolese francs. They only dealt in Congolese francs and American dollars.

And nobody ever stole their money.

Danny had told us that there was no theft in Lubumbashe. A thief would be jumped by everybody within shouting distance and beaten to death.

Danny also told us what constituted a typical traffic fine. He once saw a car double-parked illegally. Four traffic police carrying pickaxe handles waded into the car, smashed the headlights, the rear lights and all the windows. Then they tore into the bodywork, the doors and the bonnet, leaving it wrecked. Danny said that when they had finished they simply wiped their brows, and, not even waiting for the driver, walked off as if nothing had happened.

We believed him. The very next day, Matt took a short stroll around the block and witnessed a similar incident. But this one was worse. They beat the driver senseless. Matt told me a traffic policeman standing in the middle of the road blew his whistle to stop a smart 4x4 approaching him. The driver did not stop immediately, at the exact spot the policeman had indicated. The policeman and three others dragged him from the vehicle, beat him to the ground with their pickaxe handles and put the boot in.

They turned to the vehicle and gave it similar treatment.

After hearing this, I suggested to Matt that we stay in the immediate environs of Hotel Babel. Like, just stand outside for a bit of sun. Not taking any chances. He agreed.

The armed forces were volatile and potentially explosive. After decades of war, they could not be trusted.

Besides, we were told that none of them received salaries, or any pay at all. They extracted money where they could, from whom they could. Their power was also currency.

They were armed with a variety of weapons. Rifles, handguns, bayonets the length of swords, and even grenades. Matt has a degree in military science. He knows his weaponry. He identified Belgian FNs, South African army issue R1s. Ak-47s. Even South African copies of Israeli Uzzis.

'I wonder where they got those from?' he said.

There were also Tokarev pistols. Makarov pistols. Chinese stick grenades. And more.

The roller coaster plunged. Lower, because, at this time, just after midday, Goebbels had still not arrived.

He eventually arrived at 1.30 pm. We were in our room, stretched on our bed, reading, when he burst in without knocking. 'Entrée! Bonjour,' he said. 'Let's go,' he said. He herded us downstairs, out of the front door and into the coffee shop cum restaurant adjacent to the hotel. It was called the Metro Babel. He told us to be seated and to order from the menu. We ordered chicken, sadsa and Chinese cabbage. He did not stay. He paid for the meal before we received it. 'I will meet you at 6.00 pm,' he said, and left.

After lunch we stood outside the hotel and basked in the sun. Smoking, of course. Matt and I were both wearing shorts. An elderly man approached us. 'Bonjour,' he greeted us. We greeted him in French and explained that we only spoke English. He asked us our business in Lubumbashe. We told him we were missionaries. I had a cigarette stuck between my lips. He said that he would fine us for wearing shorts. He told us that he was a plainclothes policeman and demanded 10 dollars.

We pleaded poverty.

Matt also told him to fuck off in Afrikaans. He smiled and asked me to give him my packet of cigarettes. I said no and offered him one. He took two from the box. 'I will visit you later,' he smiled.

Danny joined us for a cigarette. Within minutes two Immigration Officials arrived, beckoned to Danny and escorted him up to his room. After a few minutes they returned with Danny and Rauha, climbed into a car and drove off.

Our friends returned a few hours later, alone. They told us that the officials hassled them almost every day for money. Every day they found something wrong with their passports. They were asking questions about us, Danny said. It would only be a matter of time before they paid us a visit.

'We have to get the fuck out of here, Matt.'

But of course we couldn't. We both knew that. Not yet, in any case. We had a movie to shoot. We had only enough money – in rands – to get from the border to Lusaka.

We went up to Danny's room and chatted for most of the afternoon. I imagined that if the room had been bugged we would have been shot on the spot for the content of our conversation. The three of us had spent time with the South African Defence Force in Angola. Matt had been in the permanent force, with the parabats. Danny had also served as a member of the permanent force with the infamous 32 Battalion. I had served as a conscript with a Cape Town regiment.

War stories. Matt also knew Danny's elder brother, Boesman Van Ryn. Our war stories took me back three decades, to Angola in 1976. To the mosquitoes. The flies. The Cubans. The eternal wait for the enemy to manifest itself.

* * *

By the time we arrived there, Cahama had been almost totally demolished by battling armies who seemed to change sides at the drop of a beret. Cahama was a small town in southern Angola; about 200 km northwest of Pereira de

Eca, our first point of entry into Angola after crossing the Cunene River. It was completely deserted – except for flocks of goats, stray sheep, chickens and a few emaciated dogs. Only a handful of buildings, bomb-ravaged and bullet-ridden, stood precariously amongst the ruins.

It was scorching-hot when we arrived in Cahama to set up positions to block possible Cuban / MPLA advances southward. So we were told.

We were told that we were the first 'civvy' regiment to go on active duty in a war zone outside of South African borders since the Korean war of the early 1950s. I was assigned to the 60 mm mortar section of one of the infantry platoons in this regiment. Originally trained in our teens as riflemen, all of us, apart from our mortar sergeant, were suddenly enlisted in a week's crash course in 60 mm mortars at Grootfontein, the base in the then South West Africa, where South African troops were re-trained and equipped, and from where we moved into Angola.

We spent close six weeks in and around Cahama.

Waiting for the MPLA.

Waiting for the Cubans.

Waiting for SWAPO.

The MPLA and the Cubans were our enemies. Unita were our allies. Nobody seemed to know exactly on whose side the FNLA stood.

On the way out, in late March of 1976, FNLA troops were our friends. We (their protectors?) accompanied them back to The States, as we referred to South Africa.

Unita became our enemy.

The Cubans and the MPLA remained our enemies.

It was all quite confusing.

To us, the rank and file, our real enemies were the flies and the mosquitoes. And they weren't even commies, although they were referred to often as 'fucking little black bastards.' There was never a frontal or rear attack. They surrounded

109

us totally, attacking with ease. We spent a good deal of our time planning ways to stop these monsters, against which there was little or no defence.

At the crack of dawn – referred to in military parlance as Stand To – there was perhaps a pause of a minute or so between the daily retreat of the mosquito hordes and the onslaught of the fly battalions. At dusk – Stand Down – there was the same brief pause between the withdrawal of the flies and the onslaught of the mosquitoes. At night, during the height of that blistering Angolan summer, we slept fully dressed, every millimetre of our bodies covered and wrapped in ponchos, balaclavas and tucked and zipped into sleeping bags.

And still the mossies attacked.

Breaking every rule of warfare (bush, conventional or other), we built huge log fires that would burn throughout the night, and slept beside these. Just far enough away so as not to be incinerated, yet close enough to keep the enemy at bay.

It worked, more or less. The odd special forces mossies got through and wreaked their bloody havoc on us. Then our platoon commander got cold feet and put a stop to it. Fire would give away our positions, he said. Fair enough.

But, because we were so bored, frustrated and angry with the waiting, the anxiety and anticipation of impending attacks by the other armies, terrified by thoughts of pitched battles, fire-fights, hand-to-hand combat, we told him we couldn't give a fuck. Either way, we insisted, let's get our part in this fucking war over so we can be dead or go back home. Where we actually belonged.

Letters from home – when we got them – informed us that we were actually in South West Africa, and nowhere near Angola. Letters home were handed in unsealed and rigorously censored. The powers that be did not want to alarm our families. So they lied to our families.

One night, way after midnight, all hell broke loose. A gunner manning one of the two Ratels assigned to our platoon went 'bossies,' or 'bos-befok' (literally meaning 'bush fucked,' the word describes the many white South African soldiers who lost their mental stability in the Angolan war) and opened fire on the mossies with a 7,62 mm Browning machine gun. Most of us were dead asleep. We awoke, petrified, to the chilling, rocketing sounds of whistling rounds with an awesome display of tracer bullets pouring into the black sky, lighting it up in a fluorescence of green and pink.

'YOU MOTHER-FUCKING MOSSIE BLACK BASTARDS ...' he screamed.

'YOU MOTHER ...'

And kept firing until a couple of troops close to the Ratel, who had quickly assessed the situation, clambered up onto the vehicle and pulled him down. He had to be forcibly restrained.

The rest of us thought that we were finally being attacked. Without any clear orders in the midst of the chaos, some froze where they were sleeping or standing guard, some fled from the scene far into the dark bush to take shelter and wait for the shit to subside and go away.

Just go away. Please.

Some were so pissed, they missed the fireworks. The adrenalin rush.

The next day the gunner was taken to a field hospital. We heard later that he had been sent back to The States and into a psychiatric ward at No 1 Military Hospital in Pretoria.

That's how powerful the mossie army was.

The flies were no different. There was simply no defence against them – except for one little strategy that drew them off, for a few moments at least. Unfortunately you needed to have a crap. It worked like this: covered in flies and dying for a crap, you would go a little way into the bush, some distance away from your existing position, dig a hole, drop your webbing, drop your rods; do your thing. Then slowly lift the rods, fasten the webbing, buckle up, grab rifle and spade, and sprint as fast as you can away, away, from a pile of shit writhing in flies.

A few moments of bliss.

Until the next wave of attack.

Meanwhile, we waited in vain for the Cubans, the MPLA, SWAPO.

But they never arrived.

Apart from the foot patrols on which we were sent from time to time – out into the hinterland, scouting for possible enemy positions or movement – it was an

111

excruciatingly boring existence.

Until one morning there was an urgent call to action.

The entire company was summoned to a parade. We were informed that a certain General would be inspecting our positions. We were ordered to clean our dirty selves up — some hadn't washed for weeks — launder our browns, render our assortment of weapons spotless and in perfect working order, and generally clean and tidy up our trenches and positions. There was a lot of excitement; at least the troops could look forward to a little break from the monotony; the boredom; the inertia. Maybe even have a braai and some beer. The rest of that day, and half that night, we went about the business of carrying out our orders.

The next day, as promised, the General arrived with an entourage of officers. Our mortar section stood to attention beside our spotless positions. Everything was in perfect order. The General exchanged a few words with our mortar sergeant and proceeded with his inspection. Already the flies were probing and penetrating.

After the General and his officers had scrutinised our persons and our weapons — R5s, mortar tubes, base-plates, crates of mortar bombs — a young, squeaky-clean lieutenant stopped and stood before me. In a lowered voice he asked, 'Are you guys 60 mm mortars?'

'No lieutenant,' I answered with a straight face, and standing stiffly to attention. 'Rigor Mortis.'

He smiled wryly. And moved on, following the General, the other officers, and a fast-gathering army of flies.

* * *

Strangely, neither Matt nor I noticed a single fly anywhere during our stay in the Congo. Just hordes of bloodthirsty mosquitoes. Bigger and fatter than any I had ever encountered in Angola.

Sitting in the room, talking to Matt and Danny, I thought about Angola. It was like the Congo in many ways. The waiting. The anticipation. The uncertainty. The fear.

An uncomfortable, challenging, excruciating war of nerves.

I never really came close to action in Angola in the four months I was there. The only incoming fire I experienced was while out on a manoeuvre in Grootfontein, in the then South West Africa. Our platoon was hit by the outer reaches of mortar fire from our own 90 mm mortars. Zing ... Zing ... we heard the familiar sounds of shrapnel scorching the earth and we scrambled aboard our vehicles and up surrounding trees, as high and as quickly as we could climb. That's the drill when you come under mortar fire. Get off the ground, and as high as you can. I clutched the higher branches of a nearby tree, pissing involuntarily in my browns.

Both Danny and Matt had seen a lot more action. Some of it painful and horrific. After all, they were professional soldiers. I was a civilian conscript doing a compulsory four month camp.

Real man. Toy soldier.

* * *

My four days in the Congo made my Angola journey look like a walk in the park.

Every time we heard footsteps in the corridor we thought about the immigration officials. Chilling thoughts.

Throughout our stay in the Congo, I carried at least two one-litre water bottles with me. And wherever I could, I would fill them up with tap water; throw in a water purification tablet, shake, and wait ten minutes before drinking. We had no money for coffee, cool drinks or bottled water. Danny and Rauha let us fill the bottles from their basin tap whenever they were around. The water was murky brown. Before we could drink it though, we would have to pour out some of the water. Little maggot-type insects always floated to the top. I, particularly, drank litres of water every day. My mouth was always parched and dry.

Dirty, purified water. We lived on the stuff.

That and nicotine.

Goebbels arrived at 6.30 pm. We were bundled into the RTIV staff car and taken to the main church where we interviewed personnel working for the church's radio and TV station. There was a huge transmitter – about 30 metres high – right next to the church. We shot images of it from every angle. The shoot lasted less than two hours and we were bundled back into the car and taken to the hotel. When we arrived, Goebbels got out of the car with us. He looked at me strangely. 'I will accompany you to your room. We need to talk.'

We entered the room. He and Matt sat on the edge at the foot of the bed and I squatted on the floor, my back leaning against the wall.

'I am concerned about you as Christians.' He looked me in the eye. 'How is your faith, Mr. Mario?'

'I'm a Christian, but I am also a human and sometimes weak.'

He turned to Matt and asked the same question. I don't remember Matt's response. I was furious that Goebbels was questioning us. I tried to control my anger – one wrong move and we could be thrown to the wolves. Already we were having an unhappy time of it. One cup of coffee in the last two days, and two small meals. Stuck between our dungeon, Danny and Rauha's room, the smoking-toilet and a bit of sunshine outside the front of the hotel. When Goebbels left we agreed. No more walking about the dangerous streets of Lubumbashe.

Chapter
Eleven

I was managing Swannees clothing store in Wynberg, Cape Town, in the early 1970s. One afternoon one of the sales staff placed that afternoon's *Cape Argus* on my desk. The headline read: FIRE DESTROYS BOYS' TOWN. It was accompanied by a picture.

I had left Boys' Town in 1968, after a stay of seven years. I felt a twinge of sadness at the story, which said the fire had been started by a disgruntled old boy, who was now in custody and who would soon stand trial. No name was mentioned, as the incident was *sub judice*. I could not imagine who would have done such a thing, or why.

Just before I locked up the shop for the day I received a call from John Hayward, Deputy Principal at Boys' Town when I was there. He also coached rugby, supervised cross-country running and grilled us during daily PT sessions. Hayward was a taskmaster – an ex-officer in the British Army who had served in Britain's Burmese war. He was tall and an extremely well-built and tough man who always maintained the bearing of an English officer. At this time, he was head of Public Relations for Boys' Town, South Africa, and led an army of fund-raisers, mostly women, for the cause. Boy's Town was expanding nationwide.

Hayward asked if I had read about or heard the news about the fire, and went on to say what a 'damn tragedy' it was and that he had called a press conference in Claremont for the following day. Could he and Boys' Town call on my help to put out this 'little public-relations-fire'? I said yes, without hesitation. He agreed to fetch me the next day, about an hour before the meeting when, he said, he would give me all the details.

It was Nathan 'Boetie' van Rensburg who had started the fire, Hayward said, adding that Boetie had arrived at Boys' Town a day or two before the fire, stoned and drugged out of his mind. He was causing trouble and was evicted from the school property by the boys themselves. But Boetie stole back late the next night, under cover of darkness, and set the thatched roof of the main building alight. Most of the boys had lost their possessions in the fire; and in fact, Hayward said, it was a miracle that nobody had been injured or burnt to death.

I could not believe it. Boetie? Boetie would never harm a fly. Boetie was a cool guy, and although younger than me, he had been one of my best friends while I was there. He was an extremely talented guitarist who composed his own songs. Since he was not very literate I used to write the lyrics. In fact, one of our teachers had sent a tape of his compositions to a famous South African duo, who later visited Boetie, and Boys' Town, and who complimented him on his work.

There was talk that they were interested in recording a few of his songs.

No, no, not Boetie, I thought.

Boetie had sharp blue eyes and straight blonde hair. He was always quiet and gentle. I thought of him as a 'production-line' baby (I coined the phrase). Boetie was found one morning alongside a milk bottle, wrapped in a dirty blanket on a step outside a flat in Hillbrow.

He was no more than a few weeks old. From there his journey to a succession of foster parents and children's homes began, until he landed at Boys' Town. Boetie was never a problem. I knew that. To this day, I'll swear by that.

I said this to John Hayward. 'These are the facts,' he replied. 'Accept them.'

The meeting convened and for the life of me I cannot remember most of it. I had been introduced as a model student, an ex-Mayor who knew Boetie well, and now an upstanding member of society and successful clothing store manager.

I had been primed to speak about the Boys' Town system, its ethos and attributes. Questions were fired at me from all directions. When I was lost for a spontaneous answer, Hayward would quickly answer for me.

If only John Hayward knew how much marijuana I was smoking at the time, how much I was drinking, and, like the proverbial convent-girl-let-loose, exactly how rabidly I was enjoying the fruits that had been denied me all my youth. These thoughts occurred to me repeatedly during the conference.

After the meeting, Hayward thanked me profusely. I had obviously created a very good impression.

But the meeting, the fire, Boetie, stopped me in my tracks. From that moment, I started reflecting on my past. And I never stopped. That was the day I began to question the many things that I had shrugged off as part of life. Others have experienced far worse. Let the past be. Forget it. You did what you did to survive it all. Etc. Etc.

* * *

I arrived at Magaliesburg Station by train from Johannesburg in early January of 1962, with an assortment of boys of all ages from many parts of the country.

I was from Bloemfontein. I was twelve years old, turning thirteen in June of that year. I had spent the previous nine years at Nazareth House in Kimberley, 160 km from my home in Bloemfontein, from where I was now being transferred to Boys' Town.

I was filled with apprehension and excitement. The few Nazareth House boys who had the privilege of going on to Boys' Town (others, some of my close friends, were, for one reason or another, sent to various industrial schools around the country) told glowing stories about this wonderful farm school with rolling hills, cattle, sheep, horses, and all the things that could make a young boy happy. Crucially, Boys' Town would be a change from the high walls and jail-like surrounds of Nazareth House, which was an orphanage and old-age home in one.

An open lorry was waiting to meet us. A few older boys mobilised us and herded us onto the back of the lorry with our meagre belongings. I carried a small brown suitcase that contained all my possessions.

We headed off through the tiny village of Magaliesberg — which consisted of a garage, a church with a tall thin steeple, a bottle store and a few shops — onto a narrow dirt road, to our new home. A few of the boys were singing 'We're home, because we're home, because we're home, because we're home,' to the tune of *Auld Lang Syne*. In the near distance was a mountain, on top of which — a few of the boys made sure to point out proudly — was a crude wooden cross. The boys themselves, they said, had cut down two tall poplar trees which grew next to the river at the rugby field, and assembled them into a cross which they dragged up the rocky slopes of the mountain where it was now sturdily positioned, towering over the valley below. The cross was a beacon that symbolised Boys' Town. (If you're ever in Magaliesberg and you're looking for Boys' Town, head in the direction of the cross on the mountain. The cross stands on the mountain to this day; although the old poplar tree cross has since been replaced by a stainless steel one.)

The lorry stopped a few metres from a long, narrow farm gate and a few of the boys jumped off and, jostling with each other, opened it. There were only a few new boys amongst the group. There were no more than 60 boys in my first year.

At this time Boys' Town was just four years old. It had been founded by Father Orsmond in 1958, on the grounds of the St. James Mission station, where a school run by the Oakford Dominican Sisters had been closed because of the Group

Areas Act. The Dominican Sisters supported Father Orsmond in establishing Boys' Town.

We jumped from the back of the lorry and immediately, orders were barked at us. 'Quiet! Stand in three rows, the smallest to the tallest, from left to right.' We organised ourselves into three rows, with our belongings at our feet. I saw no nuns or adults or teachers. The orders were being given by the older boys. Already I knew that Boys' Town was a special school, run and managed by the boys themselves. The teachers lived in their own homes on their farms or smallholdings, away from Boys' Town, and only came to teach and to take sport.

After a few minutes of pupils' silence, a large man (over 6 foot tall and very fat) puffing at a cigarette approached us with a smile and introduced himself as Father Orsmond. He was casually dressed. There was a chorus of friendly greetings and banter from many of the boys. 'Hello Father.' 'Nice to be home, Father.' 'How were your hols, Father?' I was immediately in awe of him. Father Orsmond greeted most of them by first name or surname and welcomed the rest of us to our new home, to Boys' Town, by shaking each one of us by the hand.

He briefly explained that he was only the principal, and that we, the boys, ran the town. He assured us new boys that we would soon get to know the ropes. He cracked a few jokes with some of the boys, and pointed a finger at one or two as if saying: 'I know what you were up to during the holidays!'

He continued his introduction by telling the new boys, and reminding the others, that it was an honour to be chosen to attend Boys' Town. The school could only cater for 100 boys at most, and that there were many, many deserving others clamouring to be accepted.

He warned us, very subtly, but in a stern tone, that if we did not conform to the rules and abide by the principles of Boys' Town we would be transferred to other schools, such as the dreaded De Bult Industrial School in George, in the Eastern Cape, or worse, the infamous reform school in Cape Town, the Constantia School for Boys. In those days, the Constantia School for Boys was patrolled by armed guards, and was immediately adjacent to Pollsmoor Prison. It was, for all intents and purposes, a prison for problem boys.

The warning put the fear of God into me.

I liked Father Orsmond. He came across as a fair and caring father-figure, with an apparent sense of humour. I noticed that, like my own father, he always had a cigarette in his hands.

Boys' Town itself was exactly as I had heard it to be. It was made up of thatched buildings, there were lots of trees, there was a mountain overlooking the place, green fields, open spaces, a river, cows, sheep, chickens, pigs and horses. There was an incredible sense of freedom; and an incredible sense of camaraderie amongst the boys.

Even the air was fresher than other places – it tingled.

The discipline was tough; but bullying and violence were strictly forbidden.

I soon settled in. After all, I had already had nine years of a lifestyle – if you could call it that – of collective discipline at Nazareth House, where bullying was the norm and the nuns (bless some of them) had very little control of what was really happening in the ranks. At Nazareth House, if one complained to a nun, retribution would descend swiftly. We learned to keep our mouths shut and simply accept things the way they were.

At Boys' Town things were completely different. It became apparent to me that Father Orsmond knew exactly what was going on at all times. The system was such that he had total control of all of us, at all times. In years to come, I often heard him say: 'I know such and such about so and so ... because I have my spies.' He would say it with a sly chuckle.

I learned the ropes well. I liked the idea that, if I tried hard enough, fitted in and behaved myself, I would have a fair chance to climb the ladder and become Mayor one day.

When one arrived at Boys' Town one was automatically a third-class citizen, right at the bottom of the hierarchy. After a period of good behaviour, one became a second-class citizen. And, if one showed exemplary behaviour, one was elevated to first-class citizenship. From there onwards, you could proceed to a position of power.

Firstly, one becomes a 'cop,' or a policeman – responsible for escorting problem boys to class, to church, to meals, to and from the lock-ups, and generally patrolling and keeping law and order. Cops had the power of arrest, and by law they could only operate in pairs. This was a strategy to prevent cops becoming corrupted. If there were two cops constantly in attendance, chances were that one of them would inform in the event of collusion between the other cop and his charge. If a guy was a problem he was placed 'under cop' – which meant he could not go anywhere or do anything without two cops in his company. All privileges and rights were taken away. When you were 'under cop' you were not allowed to speak to anybody. Not even to the cops, unless you were asked a question. If you saw two cops idling about outside a closed toilet door, you knew their charge was inside.

From the ranks of the cops, councillors were elected. There were four councillors in all. First, Second, Third and Fourth, First being the most senior and so on. Each councillor had a specific portfolio. The First councillor had the most important portfolio, he was the Minister of Justice – and was directly in charge of, and responsible for, the cops and for law and order in the town. There were Ministers of Health, Labour, Education and Sport.

The Mayor was elected twice a year from the ranks of the councillors. Generally, to become Mayor one had to go through the mill and experience all of these portfolios. But, in some cases, a fourth councillor could, after just one term, be elected as Mayor. This was the exception rather than the rule.

The control exercised by this hierarchy was solid, non-negotiable, strict and transparent. Often 'moan meetings' were assembled whereby anybody – excepting third-class citizens and boys 'under cop' – could exercise their democratic right to complain about their superiors and take them to task. These were public meetings and if any boy in power was accused of anything (from setting a bad example to committing a crime or misdemeanour, or victimising others) he had a platform from which to publicly defend himself.

Father Orsmond knew well that the smokers amongst us had a 'habit.' Being a heavy chain-smoker himself, he understood the dynamics of the habit well. And so, the privilege of smoking (only for boys sixteen years and older) was granted on merit. Boys had to be first-class citizens or higher to smoke. Banning boys from smoking was also used as an effective means of punishment. Smokers were only allowed three pipes full of tobacco a day under controlled conditions: at certain times, and only at a certain place, which was the designated smoking area. And no cigarettes were allowed.

If boys needed to sort out personal battles, after supper on a Sunday night we would all assemble in the hall next to the furrow by the bottom dormitory block, and whoever challenged whomever – and only on acceptance by both parties – the boxing gloves would come out, and a fair fight, properly refereed, with three-minute rounds like a boxing match, would follow.

The exceptional thing about Boys' Town was the calibre of the teachers. Only one nun taught us, and only a few of us at that, because she taught Latin. Her name was Sister Adrian. There were two curricula: Academic and Trade. The boys who did not display an aptitude for the classics did the basic subjects, English, Science, Afrikaans and Math, Woodwork and Motor Mechanics. The academics studied Latin, History, Geography and Biology as well as the basics. I was an academic, although I failed to grasp Math and Science, and, in my later grades, refused to study these subjects. Which is why I spent a total of four years in standards nine and ten. I got no marks for math or science because I did not write the exams. I sat the exams, and in both cases drew a line through my answer sheets, folded my arms on my desk and went to sleep. I believe to this day that I was passed simply to get me out of the system.

The teachers were mostly farmer-teachers from outlying farms, except for Mr. Cranston, our Math teacher (we called him Wally), John McIntosh, who taught English and Michael Guittard, our Geography teacher and rugby coach. Wally lived in a little self-contained cottage next to the library, adjacent to the bottom buildings. He was our censor-in-chief. All letters home were stuffed into the letterbox outside Wally's cottage, and he would read and censor them. All letters from home were also censored by Wally. One day somebody stuffed his letterbox with cow dung, and as he automatically put his hand in to take out the letters, he gathered instead a handful of fresh dung. The story became legendary and was passed on to new generations of boys. Wally would often re-tell the story himself. 'And when I put my hand into the letterbox to take out your letters, what did I get ...!'

John McIntosh and Michael Guittard lived together in a charming stone cottage on a smallholding adjoining the Boys' Town property, alongside the Magalies River. Nobody ever said it aloud, but there were whispers that the two of them were 'queer.' Not once, whilst I was at Boys' Town, or after I had left, did I hear of any incident of molestation – not even a hint – involving them. They were caring, compassionate men and nurtured talent whenever and wherever they found it in the boys. They were simply homosexuals living very happily together.

John McIntosh was not a trained teacher. He had worked as a sub-editor for *The Star* newspaper, Johannesburg's most prominent daily of the time, and had been banned by the security police, having been labelled an agitator. Somehow, he had been given special permission to teach at Boys' Town. He was basically under house arrest, and was not allowed to have more than a specified number of people at his home at any one given time. He was a brilliant English teacher, and nurtured in me a lifelong love for the works of Herman Charles Bosman.

He would also expose us – mainly the matric students – to banned books like *Catcher in the Rye*. His last English period of every week was devoted to these devious literature lessons. He went on to publish a book, *The Thorn Trees*, whilst I was still there, and later a book called *The Stone Fish*, which won the CNA Literary award – posthumously. He died in his early forties, after I had left Boys' Town. Cancer of the pancreas.

Then there was Mr. de Kok, who taught Afrikaans, and who had a farm next to Boys' Town where he grew peaches and kept a few livestock. We called him 'Kokkie.' He was a firebrand, an Afrikaner to the core and a member of the extreme right wing Afrikaner political party, the HNP, and he made no bones about it. I remember him once wading into a boy who refused to learn Afrikaans and who had called the language 'childish kitchen Dutch.' A few boys in the class had to restrain Kokkie, but only after he had landed a good few slaps and punches.

I liked Kokkie because he too was fair.

And there was Mr. Steenkamp, our science teacher, who farmed about twenty kilometers away from the school, in Hekpoort. Mr. Steenkamp was in his late sixties when I was there. He had a yellowing moustache and chain-smoked during class. He was a gentle, patient and very interesting man. It upset him that I showed no interest in science, but he did not victimise me for it. On the contrary, he tried to gain my interest in science through literature, and lent me extracts from a book written by Eugene Marais: *The Soul of the White Ant*.

'This may give you some respect for science,' he said. 'And,' he added, 'even great literary figures like Eugene Marais used science as a basis for their works.' Still, he couldn't sway my determination not to take part in his science classes. And he left it at that.

The two teachers who taught woodwork and motor mechanics were a father and son team, Mr. du Toit, Senior, and Mr. du Toit, Junior. We called them big Toytjie and little Toytjie. Neither of them was little. They both towered over six feet tall. They were real farmers, and typical Afrikaners; large, salt-of-the-earth men. Little Toytjie was also the farm manager. He taught us horsemanship, and since I was a 'horse-boy' – in charge of the horses – and a rider, I worked a lot with little Toytjie. Big Toytjie took no nonsense and on one occasion took a horse whip to one of the boys who had given him a hard time.

The most unusual of all the teachers was Father Patrick, who taught religious studies. Father Patrick was a moSotho priest who primarily ministered to the black people of the St. James mission, though he became quite involved with us, alternating with Father Orsmond in saying mass at our chapel. I was at one stage head sacristan, so I got to know him better than most. Like Kokkie, he too was a firebrand, but for different reasons. He was a short, quiet and intense man who took life very seriously, though he sometimes showed a sharp sense of humour.

One day he walked into the matric class – there were only about eight of us – obviously very angry, dumped his books on the desk and turned to the blackboard. He scribbled the word IMMORALITY on the blackboard. He turned to us, eyes glowing, and almost spitting out his words, shouted: 'Tell me the meaning of this word!'

There was a deathly silence amongst us. Then one of the guys, Leon Mortensen, casually answered, 'Sleeping with a black woman,' followed by an audible chuckle from somebody else.

All hell broke loose. Father Patrick flung the chalk wildly into our midst, and raising his voice just lower than a scream, ordered, 'Get out your fucking Oxfords, or your Websters, or any fucking dictionary you have and look up the word immorality!' Almost immediately, calmness overcame him, and, looking directly at me, he asked: 'What does it say?'

I had opened my Oxford dictionary and turned to the appropriate page, nervously looking for the word, and then read its definition: 'The lowering of moral standards ... Father ...'

'Thank you,' he said. He wiped the word from the blackboard, instructed us to turn to the correct page in one of the religious studies books we had been working through, and continued with the lesson. Not another word was ever said.

I would often accompany Father Patrick to Lady Ina Oppenheimer's 'Bluebird Farm' in Hekpoort, about an hour's drive from the school, where he would say mass from time to time. Lady O – this was what we affectionately called her – had become a Catholic and had built a beautiful little stone chapel on her farm. She was also Boys' Town's major patron and benefactor. The main classroom and dormitory block at Boys' Town was named the Oppenheimer Wing.

Father Patrick and Father Orsmond took turns saying mass at the little chapel on Lady O's farm.

Whenever Lady O was at the farm, Father Orsmond would say mass – that's because after mass he and I, (or whoever was head sacristan and Boys' Town ambassador at the time) would go down to the main house, the mansion alongside the man-made lake built by the late Sir Ernest Oppenheimer, for a sumptuous lunch with many of Lady O's Johannesburg friends and family; the extremely rich. I met Harry Oppenheimer at Bluebird Farm on two occasions, and was a guest, with Father Orsmond, when Lady O hosted a do for Mary Oppenheimer on her engagement to Gordon Waddell, the former British Lions rugby player. I remember Mary Oppenheimer being the last to arrive at the function, and the first to leave. I found that quite strange. I liked her car. It was a posh red convertible sports model.

When Father Patrick conducted the mass, with me assisting as altar boy, we went afterwards for lunch to the home of Lady O's personal chef, a lovely lady, whose name I forget. The meals were always just as sumptuous – sans the wines and the rich Johannesburg friends.

Always, on our way to and from the farm, at least a half a dozen times a year over a period of about three years, Father Patrick and I would discuss politics, apartheid, and the dismal state of the country. We had a little game going where we would plot the overthrow of the Pretoria government. We always ended up laughing our heads off. If the authorities at the time knew that a black priest was ministering to the souls and minds of white boys, Boys' Town would have been in trouble. Black people were not allowed to operate in positions such as these. But I considered myself lucky, in fact blessed. Father Patrick had awakened my conscience and the rebel in me. Many boys, when we debated black-white relations and apartheid, called me a 'kaffirboetie.' I was not troubled, generally, because, by then, I was already part of the governing echelon of boys. Power was on my side.

Father Patrick proved to be one of the most important influences on my life and future thinking. Well into my fifties, I still use him as a reference point when my conscience troubles me.

Father Reginald Orsmond, though, had the most lasting, most powerful influence on my life. He was a brilliant man, unpretentious and with a razor-sharp mind and sense of humour to match. It was he who taught me the meaning of the word tolerance, long before I could even spell it.

Having been in children's homes since just after the age of three, never really knowing my own father, I looked to Father Orsmond as a colossal father figure. Not just because of his size, but because of the immense wisdom and authority he carried and showed. I saw in him only love and concern for the well-being of the boys. He was no softie though. He handled fire with fire, and having tried as hard as he could to transform a boy and turn him into a model citizen, without success, not easily giving up, he would eventually admit defeat and the boy in question would immediately be transferred to another school.

He always stressed that there was no such thing as a problem boy. There were only problem parents, he insisted. He stressed too that every boy, every person, was inherently good. His challenge, he said, was to help boys transform their negative energy into positive energy. I certainly believed that. I was at Boys' Town not because I was a 'bad' boy. I was just unfortunate to have come from a broken home, with an alcoholic father. Some of the boys even referred to him affectionately as 'Big Daddy.' Even today, in 2006, I know one or two ex-Boys' Town boys who still remember him as Big Daddy, long after his death.

One day, during the first part of my first year, before the midyear holidays, I was in bed with a bout of flu. To get off school and duties, and to stay in bed for a day or more, was not easy to accomplish. The nuns would rigorously check you out, and if castor oil (the nuns' remedy for most ailments, short of obviously broken limbs or wounds) did not work, there was no improvement and you had a temperature, they would concede that you were indeed sick, that you were not faking, and confine you to bed for a day or two.

I really was sick, with a roaring temperature, and I was alone in the bedroom.

It was before lunch, I remember, when Father Orsmond came into the room and enquired after my health. He was smoking as usual. He stood at the foot of my bed and began asking me how I liked being at Boys' Town. I admitted that I was very happy, and sorry to be sick. He asked me about my years at Nazareth House. I told him that they were fine but I was much happier to be at Boys' Town. He then said that he had received a written report about me from the Mother Superior at Nazareth House. And that certain aspects worried him a little. I was confused. I had never caused trouble at Nazareth House. He went on to say that it was stated in the report that I had the tendency to 'play' with other boys. I was dazed. I really was. I wanted to climb out of my bed and run as far away as I could. I started to deny the accusation. He told me to be quiet. 'Maybe you were never the perpetrator (he always used these big words), but you certainly, as far as I am led to believe, were part of certain acts,' he said.

I was thirteen years old. I had no way of countering this accusation; no way of mustering any defence at all. At Nazareth House, I knew never to complain to the nuns. It was an unwritten code that what happened amongst the boys stayed amongst the boys. No matter how degrading, how painful the experience. I was too young, too naïve to know then just how powerfully manipulative Father Orsmond really was.

I tried to explain to him that I had had only two or three experiences – against my will, I protested – when he suddenly said, 'don't worry, I'll take your word for it.' He added that I was an incipient alcoholic. 'A what?' I thought to myself. 'What do you mean, Father?' I asked. He told me that it meant I was prone to alcohol abuse because it ran in my family; it was a condition just waiting to be activated. Then he left the room. I was shaken and disturbed, and overcome by an incredible guilt. Why did I allow those things to happen to me? Why did I not have the guts to speak out against the bigger boys? Why did I keep quiet? Am I an alcoholic?

My chances of making a success of myself at Boys' Town, of becoming Mayor one day, were gone. I put my head under the pillow and sobbed.

The mid-year holidays came and went. We never had our mid-year holidays at the same time as other schools. It was a strategy to keep us away from the influence of our peers back home. I passed my first year exams. Within my first year I also became a first-class citizen. The Christmas holidays came and went. I was into my second year at Boys' Town, and loving it.

I was going places. The day Father Orsmond had confronted me in my sick-bed was long forgotten. It was nearly mid-year holidays again. I would turn 14 in June. The rugby season had started and I had been picked to play fly-half for the under 15s, which was not such a big deal at Boys' Town – there were so few of us that fifteen-year-olds often even played for the first team, along with a few twenty-year-olds!

Once a month, on the last Saturday of every month, we were treated to a movie. It was the highlight of the month. Our driver, Thomas, who worked for the mission station as well as for Boys' Town, would drive the lorry or the school bus (which Lady O had donated) and, accompanied by one of the councillors, or even the Mayor, go to Krugersdorp to fetch the film, which came in two or three metal reels.

Father Orsmond loved movies and would often decide what we would watch. Sometimes he'd let the councillors decide. The school would hire a projector, which would be set up in the hall. At the bottom of the hall was a stage, where we held end-of-year concerts for teachers, the nuns, other staff, and in some cases, visiting dignitaries, like Lady O. A big sheet was hung as a screen on the back wall of the stage.

Father Orsmond always operated the projector, unless he was away. This Saturday night we were going to watch a western – my favourite.

I was sitting, huddled and squashed amongst my friends, right in the front row of seats – an assortment of plastic chairs and benches. As we were eagerly awaiting the beginning of the action, one of the senior boys at the back called out my name. I stood up and looked his way. He beckoned: Come here. I was surprised, and worried that I would lose my prime spot. I walked up to the boy, and he took me outside. It was mid-winter, about the end of May, and very cold. He told me that Father Orsmond wanted to see me, and that I was to go immediately. I had noticed earlier on that Father Orsmond was not in the hall, sitting next to the projector as he normally did. I thought maybe he was away.

'Where is Father?' I enquired of the boy. 'Is he in his office?.'

'No, you have to go up to his room. You are to knock on his door.'

Father Orsmond's bedroom was in the main dormitory block, between other bedrooms. 'What is it he wants with me?' I wondered to myself, hoping secretly that it would be a quick meeting and that I'd get back in time to see the movie, or at least a good part of it. I stood before the door of his room for a while, too nervous to knock. Eventually I gathered my courage and knocked on the door. Father Orsmond called from within. 'Come in, Dof.' I was called Dof, because nobody could pronounce my surname, d'Offizi. Part of the efficacy of the nickname was the fact that the word 'dof' means stupid in Afrikaans.

The door was unlocked. I opened gently and entered. The light was off, but there was light from a bedside lamp. There was an electric heater on the floor near the bed. I noticed the red-hot elements. The room, unlike the rest of the rooms in the block, was carpeted. It was spacious. The curtains were closed, hiding the bay windows of the alcove at the other side of the room.

128

There were strong smells of cats and cat piss. We all knew Father had three Siamese cats, although we rarely saw them. I saw them then, sitting up on the counter of a cabinet in the little alcove. I also noticed a few bottles of liquor next to the cats.

I took a few more paces, past a bathroom and into the room. On my right was a double bed. Father Orsmond was lying in the bed, covered by a thin white sheet, with a cigarette in his hand. He greeted me. 'Thanks for coming Dof,' he said, and bade me sit down. I walked towards a chair next to the cabinet. He stopped me and said, 'Come sit here.' He indicated to a space on his left, in the bed. I continued towards the chair.

'Dof,' he repeated, 'come sit here. I am not going to eat you.' He chuckled. He had his thick brown-rimmed glasses on. They – and the cigarettes – were his trademark.

Despite the heated room, I felt ice-cold and nervous. My legs were quivering. I sat down on the bed. He stubbed the cigarette out in the ashtray on the table next to him and immediately lit another.

I don't remember the small-talk.

Then he drew the sheet away from his upper body, down towards his legs and I saw that he was naked. He had a hard-on. I looked away quickly. I didn't want to see this. He kept smiling at me, and smoking. Lighting one cigarette after the other.

All I remember is him asking me, 'Dof, will you toss me off?'

I looked away, at the carpet, at my feet, into dead space.

'I can't, Father.'

'Why not? I won't hurt you '

'I can't, Father.' I said it over and over. I fidgeted. He persisted.

I stood up. Walked around. Sat down again. I was claustrophobic.

Then he asked if I wanted something to drink. He pointed to the liquor bottles on the cabinet behind me and said I could have what I wanted if it would help me relax. I felt as though I had been in his room for hours. Trapped. Confused.

I stood up and, robot-like, went to the cabinet. There was an assortment of liquor: whisky, brandy, rum ...

'Try the Drambuie. You might like the taste.'

I looked closely at the bottles to find the Drambuie. I had never heard of it before. I found the bottle and opened it. It had the strong smell of citrus. My hands were shaking. Without looking for a glass I took a large swig. Apart from the red wine mixed with lemonade that my father used to let me drink with spaghetti, I had never ever touched alcohol. The Drambuie was strong and burnt my lips, my tongue, my mouth and all the way down into my stomach. But I liked the taste. I took another even larger gulp. Then another.

'Take it easy, Dof,' he said.

I went back to the bed and sat down. My head started swimming and I felt nauseous. I fought the tears. Father Orsmond's hand fondled my thigh; then he reached for my fly and unzipped it. My eyes were locked on the dead space at my feet.

Then he took my hand and placed it on his penis.

The next morning I attended Sunday mass, as was compulsory for the Catholics amongst us. Father Orsmond administered Holy Communion. I kept my eyes shut tight as I tilted my head back and stuck out my tongue to receive the host. The body of Christ.

Over the next three years, from time to time Father Orsmond would summon me to his room; I slept in the top building, a few rooms from his. My bed was next to the open windows by the passage. He would come late at night and wake me up by shining a torch in my face. The dreaded light of the torch. I got to know it.

When I got out of bed and went to his room the first thing I did was go to the liquor cabinet and pour a stiff drink, without asking. I got to love the taste of Drambuie and rum. Yes, two or three large tumblers of rum and coke will do. And maybe a shot of brandy?

I refused anal sex. I refused to do anything but toss him off. This clearly frustrated him. But no amount of alcohol would change it. So, I would lie back and fantasise about girls, especially Cathy Hayward – John Hayward's daughter – who spent her holidays and weekends at Boys' Town. She was blonde and beautiful and all the boys had a crush on her, especially when she came to swim at the pool.

I fantasised about some of the girls I had met back home during the holidays. And I fantasised about Father Orsmond's niece, Pamela, who had 'black, doe-large eyes set in an assertive face of milk-white prettiness ...' as I had once written on a piece of paper, my first ever *haiku*, which I had slipped to her after mass one Sunday morning. I would lie there, my head swimming in rum and Drambuie, and Father Orsmond would ravish me at will. No kissing on the lips, I insisted.

No kissing on the lips, please, I begged him.

I was a flat, immoveable, inflexible stretch of canvas on which he lustfully indulged his desires.

Strangely, I felt compassion at times. Mostly I felt disgust and overwhelming, incredible guilt. He was a large man and his weight, and the intensity of his sucking and biting would often hurt me. But the alcohol helped me handle it. And, I reassured myself, over and over, it will pass, it will stop; it will all go away sometime soon.

Every session was followed by mass and Holy Communion. Because mass was compulsory, every single day of the week.

Nobody knew or even suspected what was going on. Often I wondered if I was the only boy he was involved with. Even at this age, I knew that this was impossible. But I never laboured the thought. I was often tempted to confide in others; maybe the nuns, or Mr. McIntosh, or Mr. Guittard – I liked them both very much – but I knew from my experiences at Nazareth House that this would be fatal. I knew with certainty that I would be labelled an agitator, a problem boy, and would quickly find my way to the Constantia School for Boys in Cape Town. One holiday, I thought about telling my father. But, on second thoughts, I let it go. He would have beaten me to a pulp. To him, an Italian, an old-fashioned Catholic, there was no way on God's earth that a priest like Father Orsmond – or any priest for that matter – could or would commit such acts. My sense of survival, finely honed in Nazareth House, told me to shut up. I was alone. Alone I would have to take the consequences of my actions.

It was one of Father Orsmond's dictums: 'You must take the consequences of your actions.' He told us this countless times.

Just before my sixteenth birthday I approached Father and told him that I loved girls and women too much, and, almost apologetically, asked for this relationship to stop. He just smiled at me.

And it never happened again. I noticed that whenever the subject of girls came into a discussion with him, and other boys and I showed interest and enthusiasm, he would make a caustic remark.

Meanwhile, I climbed the ladder to the top. I was a terrible student and an average sportsman – except for horse-riding and cross country running – even though I became captain of the 1st rugby side. I was, however, popular with all the boys. I held every council position, from fourth to first, and by seventeen became Mayor. Father Orsmond, to his credit, never stood in my way. He nurtured my rise to the top. He frowned, however, at the fact that I was too popular. He once told me that popularity could be seen as a sign of weakness.

As head sacristan and Boys' Town ambassador I became Lady O's favourite son, and spent hours with her at Bluebird Farm after Sunday mass. After lunch, Father would rest for an hour or two and Lady O would show me her photographs – she had achieved a certain renown as a wildlife photographer. She would talk to me on many subjects, always encouraging my opinions and point of view. She taught me a great deal about life, and how the other half lived. She became a nurturing mentor.

On one occasion, a few weeks before my final matric exams, while we were sitting down to lunch with more than a dozen other guests, Father Orsmond asked Lady O if he could make a small announcement. We all sat back and gave him our attention.

He said, smugly, 'Lady O, Dof is going to give you a wonderful Christmas present.'

She looked at me in surprise. 'What sort of present, Dof?' she asked.

Father Orsmond answered, 'Dof is going to get a first class matric!'

She replied, looking directly at me with a beautiful smile, countering Father Orsmond, 'Don't worry about a first class matric, Dof – just keep on writing lovely poetry.' I felt as if I had won a major battle. I didn't look to see Father Orsmond's reaction.

Earlier that year I had undergone an IQ test, as all boys did sometime or another before leaving the school. Soon after this test I asked Father Orsmond if he could tell me my results. In those days your IQ was the finite measurement of your intellect, intelligence and potential. He said that he was not allowed to disclose the results. 'Come on, Father, tell me. Nobody will know but you and me,' I jibed.

He looked at me, meanness layered behind his smug smile. 'Let's say that it is bordering on the average.' Then he added. 'I won't say which side of average.'

I was devastated. I have never forgiven him.

And yet, I grew to love Boys' Town. It was the only real home I had. One Christmas holiday I missed my friends so much I ran away from home a few days before Christmas day and hitch-hiked back to Boys' Town. I wanted to join those who stayed there for the holidays because they had nowhere else to go.

It was one of the best Christmases of my life. We would spend our days, including early mornings at sunrise, riding horses. There were five horses in all. I had a horse in my care, Jagger, whom nobody was allowed to ride without my permission during the time I was in charge of the horses (my last three years). We would also take long walks through the neighbouring farms, along countless dirt roads; we would climb the mountain and surrounding hills and, of course, raid Kokkie's peach orchard, right under his nose.

Towards the end of my last year – my second year in standard ten – Pamela, father Orsmond's niece, begged me to teach her to ride properly. She told me that her mother said it was okay. I knew she had a crush on me. I was 18. She was 15. I agreed, very happily.

Her grandparents, Father Orsmond's mother and father – whom we called Ma and Pa Orsmond – lived in a big stone house a short distance from the stables. Pamela went to a convent in Krugersdorp and came home each weekend and during the holidays.

Father Orsmond gave me permission to give Pamela riding lessons.

Almost immediately we grew infatuated. We declared undying love.

At night, when she was home, after our lights-out, I would dress, sneak out of my bedroom and jog to her house. She had a room adjoining the main house. I would knock on the window and she'd join me outside. No matter how cold the weather, we'd make our way across the fields and to the river. We'd lie on the grassy banks. We always took a blanket.

We'd hug and kiss and play until the early hours of the morning, when I would take her back home and run ecstatically down the dirt tracks, taking a short cut through the donga and across the lucerne fields, back to my room. I was never caught. I believed nobody knew or suspected. Many years later, a good friend of mine, Alan Hearn, told me that he and another friend, Alfie, knew about my relationship with Pamela. In fact, he said, they waited for me to leave before they bounded off in the opposite direction, to Kokkie's farm to meet his daughter.

Pamela and I never had full sex. My father, on one of the very few occasions I was with him, gave me a little old-fashioned advice. If you break a young girl's virginity, the honourable thing to do is to marry her. I remembered it.

My visits to Pamela became more frequent. Every time she was home we would meet. We also became complacent and dropped our guard. Instead of going to the river, I would creep into her bed with her. Pamela smoked. I never did, and I always warned her that maybe, just maybe, one of her grandparents would pass the room, smell tobacco smoke and bust us.

The night before my last matric exam, I was with Pamela in her room. We heard the shuffling of feet outside. Then a knock on the door. It was Ma Orsmond. 'Are you smoking in there Pamela?' she asked.

'No, Gran,' Pamela replied in a raised, slightly fearful voice. There was a brief silence and then we heard the doorknob turn. Pamela had bolted the door. 'Why is your door locked? Open up!' demanded Ma Orsmond. Pamela and I looked at each other, wide-eyed. There was nowhere to hide.

'Open this door!' Ma Orsmond demanded.

I dressed quickly. Pamela unbolted and opened the door. Ma Orsmond entered. She gasped and held her hands to her mouth.

'We did nothing, Ma!' I blurted out instinctively.

'Get out of here,' she said. 'Get out!'

Without saying goodbye, I scuttled from the room and jogged breathlessly down the dirt road to Boys' Town. I clearly remember a full, bright moon lighting my way – which saved me from stumbling and falling; that's how fast and thoughtlessly I ran.

When I got back to Boys' Town I went straight to Father Orsmond's room. On the run back I decided that I would be the first to tell him.

I stood outside his door for a long while, mustering all the courage I could for the drama I knew would unfold. Father Orsmond's dictum recurred. 'Always take the consequences of your actions.'

I lifted my fist to knock, then I chickened out. And waited, again and again, for an eternity. Then I knocked, softly at first. Then louder, and louder. I heard Father Orsmond calling from within. 'Who is it?'

'Its me, Dof, Father,' I called out.

I heard a shuffle and movement from within. The door had been locked. Father Orsmond opened. It was way past midnight. He looked at me, still half asleep, and asked what on earth was happening.

'I need to speak to you, Father,' I stammered. He invited me into his room.

I told him that I had something important to tell him and asked if we could go to his office. I remember a look of mystification on his face. He told me to wait outside his office while he got dressed. My palms were wet with sweat. He met me outside his office, opened up, went in, and sat behind his desk. I sat in a chair across from him.

He said something to the effect of, 'Well, what is it Dof, that can't wait until the morning?'

He looked at his watch and asked me if I knew what time it was.

'Father, I have something to tell you,' I blurted out.

'Well, go ahead.'

'I can't.'

'Well, you're going to have to, aren't you?'

'Father ...' pause ... 'I can't tell you.'

He looked at his watch again, and said, 'Well in a few short hours I have to get up to say mass, so we can sit here until you do tell me.'

I sat in stony silence for quite a long while. He lit cigarette after cigarette. Then I suddenly blurted it out. 'Ma caught me with Pamela tonight.' I spilt the words out as quickly as I could.

I was astounded by his reaction.

'Did she catch you in bed with Pamela?'

'No!'

'You were in bed with Pamela, weren't you?'

'Yes,' I stammered, 'But we did nothing wrong.'

For a while he just sat and looked at me, puffing away. Then he shuffled through a pile of papers on his desk. I couldn't tell what he was looking for. He lifted his head, slowly and deliberately, looked at me and said, 'I see you are writing your last exam today, at 9.00 am. Mmm ... Latin,' he added.

'Yes, Father.'

'Extraordinary circumstances need to be treated in extraordinary ways,' he said. 'When you've finished writing your Latin paper, Thomas will take you to Johannesburg, from where you will take the train to your mother in Cape Town. I want you to say nothing to anybody. I repeat, to no one at all.'

'Are you expelling me Father?'

'In a manner of speaking, yes. But no-one need know unless you tell them. I suggest you leave with your dignity and honour intact, bearing in mind the consequences for Pamela.'

I could not believe what I was hearing, and quickly said, with some relief, 'Father, you can take Pam to the doctor, I swear we did not have sex!'

He looked at me and shook his head. 'I'm disappointed in you Dof. And I'm banning you from returning to Boys' Town to visit for at least the next two years. Good luck with your exams. Sister Clothilda will sort out your travel arrangements.' Then he stood up, and, without shaking my hand, said, 'Goodbye and get some sleep before mass.'

I left his office and went to my room. I did not sleep. Shortly after I had written my exam, Thomas, the driver, took me to Johannesburg Station, where I caught the afternoon train to Cape Town. Sister Clothilda had organised bedding and meal tickets for the trip.

I had the same little brown suitcase with which I had first arrived at Boys' Town. And R10.

I admit to being incredibly sad.

Seven years in Boys' Town had to come to this.

* * *

I was devastated by the fire at Boys' Town. And devastated that my friend Boetie had caused it. For years after the fire I wondered what made Boetie do such a drastic thing. I spoke to all the old boys I knew, and they all told me the same thing. Boetie had arrived stoned and high on acid and other drugs, and set the place alight. I had heard from many sources that the boys, when they caught him fleeing from the scene, had beaten him up before he was arrested by the police. Perhaps this was understandable. When you became loyal to Boys' Town you would fight tooth and nail to protect it. It was home and family, after all. For some boys, it was all they had.

But it niggled at me for years. Secretly, I never stopped questioning.

Why?

Why?

How close to the truth can we ever come? I persisted with my quest.

In August of 2006 I met up with an ex-Boys' Town boy for whom I had always had great respect. Years prior to this meeting, I had indicated to him that I needed to talk to him, to confide in him. I couldn't do it, though, and kept putting it off. I was not sure how he would react. What would he think of me? He was, and still is, an avid sportsman, and has become an extremely successful businessman, devout Christian, husband and father.

At the time of our meeting I was past worrying about what he would think of me. I needed to off-load. And I needed to know the truth about Boetie. I told him my dark secret, and he hugged me. He told me that his younger brother, who had died a few years earlier, had been molested by Father Orsmond. He was angry, and had been all these years. He referred to Father simply as Orsmond. On many an occasion, he told me, he had confronted Father Orsmond. He had even written to the Johannesburg Catholic Diocese and protested when Father Orsmond was ordained Bishop of Johannesburg. 'After what he had done, and the church knew about it! Instead of retiring him, they rewarded him with the position of Bishop of Johannesburg!'

His anger was barely controlled.

He told me the truth about Boetie. He had taken the trouble to find out. And he had it from reliable sources.

Boetie had gone to Boys' Town for help and refuge. He had gone there because he was in trouble and had nowhere else to go. Father Orsmond had refused to see him. Boetie was asked to leave the property. John Hayward was present – and gave his tacit approval when the boys beat Boetie.

After Boetie was arrested, Social Welfare was called in. Boetie was found unfit to stand trial and was sentenced to life at Sterkfontein, a mental institution near Johannesburg, at the State President's pleasure.

In his testimony to the police, in the presence of Social Welfare personnel, he repeatedly cried out: 'He told me he loved me! He told me he loved me! He sodomised me ... He sodomised me! He told me he loved me ...'

Chapter
Twelve

One afternoon a few of us were chatting with Father Orsmond in the commonroom. One of the boys asked Father Orsmond to explain the meaning of the word schizophrenia. He tried his best to explain, telling us that it was a progressive deterioration of the personality – an emotional instability characterised by contradictory or conflicting behaviour.

I thought about my macho image amongst the boys. I was very popular with them. Many looked up to me. I was Mayor and 1st team rugby captain. After every holiday, I would talk about the girls I had met. I was always in love with some girl or another.

Then I thought about my sexual relationship with Father Orsmond and silently cringed. On hearing his explanation of schizophrenia, I immediately assumed that I may well be schizophrenic. After all, here's macho man Mario having sex with another man.

As I was wont to do, I quickly swept the thought away. Out of my mind.

On leaving Boys' Town the thought of my being schizophrenic plagued me from time to time, always accompanied by heavy breathing, sweating, palpitations and a terrible itch on my neck, face and arms. And always, I would push the thought from my mind, reassure myself, and get on with things in the best way I could.

Soon after I married Linda, and just weeks after my first son Paul was born, I had an excruciatingly painful and confusing experience. It was late one Sunday afternoon and I was relaxing in the lounge of Linda's home, where we were living.

A feeling of sheer panic and confusion overcame me. Sweating, palpitations, difficult – almost impossible – breathing ... painful itching all over my body. I was even slightly blinded. I made my way to the kitchen where Linda was busy doing chores. Her mother, sister Marie and boyfriend John were resting. Linda saw the horror and confusion on my face and in my body language. When she asked what was wrong I could not get the words out. They just would not come. I began to shake uncontrollably. She ran to her sister Marie's room to wake her and John. When they saw my condition they bundled me into their car and sped to Victoria Hospital a short distance away. The clerk on duty in the casualty ward asked me to fill out and sign some forms. I still could not speak, and the shaking and confusion had worsened. A doctor on duty was quickly summoned.

I woke up a day later; the doctor had injected me with a powerful sedative. Before discharging me, the doctor suggested that I see my family doctor as a matter of urgency. I did not have one, but my best friend Brandon Platt's father was a doctor. Brandon arranged an appointment for me.

Dr. Manfred Platt gave me a thorough check-up and found nothing physically wrong with me. He knew a bit about my past and suggested I see a psychologist; he had a colleague whom he could recommend. I told him that I did not immediately have the money for treatment. He told me not to worry, that he would take care of it, and made an appointment for the following day.

The psychologist's rooms were somewhere on the upper floors of a skyscraper in the centre of Cape Town. I could see Table Bay and the harbour from the window. He bade me sit down opposite him, and made me feel comfortable and relaxed. I think Dr. Platt had briefed him. He asked me to relate exactly what had happened to me, and how I had felt. After which he asked me to talk about my past, and anything in particular that was worrying me. I told him about my childhood, my parents, Nazareth House and Boys' Town. I told him about Father Orsmond and our relationship. I also stressed how grateful I was to Boys' Town for the opportunity afforded me to receive care and an education.

I thought, briefly, that perhaps he himself was Catholic and would not take kindly to what I was telling him. I imagined that he could be silently diagnosing me as schizophrenic. He asked further questions and patiently coaxed me to speak without shame, or fear of judgement on his part.

It was a long, long conversation.

Then he suddenly stood up and walked around the desk a few times. He stopped behind me once, stood there and grasped my shoulder gently in his hand. He gave the back of my neck a slight rub. He walked around the desk, shaking his head from time to time. Then he went to the window and opened it.

He said, 'My boy, if I had been through just half of what you have, I would have thrown myself from this window a long time ago.' And added, 'Something you're not going to do and will never do. Because you are strong. God, you have come so far, you have endured so much, and the last thing you need is drugs or even regular counselling. Come on, you can do it. Just keep strong and leave the past where it belongs. Concentrate on your wife and child and your future.' And then he added: 'If you find it difficult to cope from here, my door is always open.'

I didn't take the elevator to the ground floor. I ran, hopped, skipped – happy and filled with renewed hope – down the many flights of stairs.

The word schizophrenia disappeared completely from my thinking.

Only many years later did the experiences of my past begin to resurface and bother me. But I quickly deflected these negative thoughts. Swept them away. Buried them deep inside myself. 'I don't want to go there … I don't want to go there.'

In my conversations with friends and colleagues, especially if they touch on the subjects of sexual and child abuse, I become visibly angry and passionate. 'Don't fuck with our children!' I say. I repeat it over and over: 'Don't FUCK with any children!'

And I have my own set of commandments, which I relate to as many people as care to listen. In my book, there are only four cardinal sins; all others are mere parking fines. ONE – Rape. Why? Because the victim lives with the trauma forever. TWO – Child abuse. Why? Because the child lives with the trauma forever, into adulthood. THREE – The neglect or abuse of talent. Why? Because the person, child or adult lives an unfulfilled life … forever. FOUR – Murder. Why is murder only at number four? Because the victim is no longer around to feel the pain.

Most people seem to agree with this thinking.

Chapter Thirteen

When Danny Hendrickse died, in the mid 80s, there was an article in one of Cape Town's daily newspapers about 'Danny Hendrickse ... Cape Town's Last Farrier ...' How Danny Hendrickse not only shoed horses, including the horses of the municipality, those big grayish-white horses that drew the municipal garbage carts in the early days, but also special racehorses from the stables of the wealthy, and how he had also been the last of the wheelwrights into his late seventies, still making and repairing wagon wheels from raw strips of metal in an old-fashioned furnace, using the timeless bellows and charcoal fires.

I remember the bellows. I used to work them for pocket money during holidays.

Uncle Danny was my mother's salvation.

I loved horses, as did he, so I felt at home in Uncle Danny's company, and that of his assistant John. I remember being extremely proud of Uncle Danny when I read the article, pleased that somebody had noticed that he had played such an important role in keeping the traditions of the past alive. Of course, apart from his love of the work and the horses, it was an occupation to Uncle Danny. He was a humble, simple man, as honest as any. He attended church every Sunday and drank very little, and very occasionally. Uncle Danny played a huge role in keeping my mother sane and hopeful. And alive. He was very generous with the money he earned each day.

Danny was a large, powerful, but gentle man. He had a short-cropped moustache and black hair that reminded me of Adolf Hitler.

'The fucking rats ...' my brother Monty would repeat this over and over again when he was drunk. He would break into raucous laughter: 'The fucking rats ... we poison them here and the bastards die next door to stink out the neighbours ...' There were eight of us living in the back room of the boarding house in Stranton Road, which ran parallel to the train line, right next to Wittebome station. The coloured people across the line called our area 'White Langa,' after the black township outside the city.

This December holiday, 1965, my mother, Uncle Danny, my sisters (Lillian and Alba), Monty and his two little girls (Erica and Pam) and I were living in that little room. My mother, Uncle Danny and Monty's little girls slept in the double bed. The rest of us took turns between the floor and the single small couch. We had a loose rotation system going. When Monty was drunk, which was often, or if it was very cold, he would sleep under the bed.

There was no fridge. We cooked on a single-plate primus stove. The washing up was done in a plastic bucket. There were two chairs, a table and an old wooden cupboard. Adjoining our room was a small passageway that led to the main house. Off the passage was a bathroom and toilet which we all shared with the neighbours from the main house.

From the room itself there was a door which opened onto the yard which was part of Uncle Danny's blacksmith shop. The horses and carts gathered there early every morning, waiting until Uncle Danny was ready to open the workshop.

Under the floorboards of our back room was a colony of rats. They came up regularly at night when we were asleep, and ate the groceries. That's why we put down the rat poison.

When I came home from Boys' Town this December holiday things had changed radically. The fact that I came at Christmas time was also different – I normally visited during the August holidays. My mother had moved from the main house. She had been evicted because she couldn't keep up the rent. Monty and Victor had put Henry on the train to Johannesburg after beating the shit out of him, once again because he was beating my mother and sisters.

Monty had left the police force and was working for the Railways. My mother was now 'sort-of-living' with Uncle Danny in the back room. Monty left the police force because he had lost the will to continue. He was patrolling outside the grounds of the State President's estate in Rondebosch with his partner when they gave chase to three men trying to scale the perimeter fence. Monty chased after one of the culprits who stopped, turned, and attacked him with a knife. Monty shot and killed him.

Soon after, he left the force. His wife left him. He took to the bottle.

Uncle Danny, at least for the first year of the relationship, would stay with my mother during the week and go home at weekends to the family home in the better part of Wynberg, where he had lived most of his life before meeting my mother. They later moved to a little room, also in Wynberg, adjacent to Kaplan's Corner Café. They had no bathroom and washed outside or in the kitchen in a large aluminium tub, boiling water in pots and the kettle.

They never married. They lived together until his death, for 18 years. It was the longest my mother had ever stayed with a man.

Not once did Danny lift his hands to her.

He was known to all as Danny the Blacksmith and he had many friends, because he had a lot of time for people. No matter their status or colour, he had time for them, as long as they showed respect for others, and animals, especially horses. My mother always said that all the stray cats in the neighbourhood would come to Uncle Danny for a small loan, food, even shelter in the workshop. On Fridays after work he'd have a glass of wine with John, his assistant, and customers and friends. One particular friend was an elderly man named Manie. Manie had horns tattooed on either side of his forehead just above his eyebrows, and looked like the devil to children. But he was far from it. He was a gentle soul and a gentle drunk. He would work the bellows some days for Uncle Danny in exchange for a couple of glasses of wine, when he was not at his full-time job in Cape Town's Government Gardens, where he tended the roses. Roses were his speciality and he said that only he was allowed to prune them in the season. Uncle Danny told me that Manie came from an aristocratic family in England. He had been badly wounded and slightly crippled in one leg during the Second World War and he suffered from severe shell shock. Manie was often incoherent, even when he was dead sober. Uncle Danny told me that after the war his parents shipped him off to distant relatives in Cape Town. On his way home some nights, when he was too drunk to continue his journey, Manie would come through the side entrance by the passage and the bathroom, and sleep in the bathroom or on the passage floor.

We always left the door open and a blanket for him, just in case.

One night one of us locked the door by mistake. The next day, on his way to work, my brother found Manie lying out in the open on a wooden bench, on the platform of Wittebome Station, across the way from us. The previous night had been very stormy. Monty tried to wake the sleeping Manie, but he was dead. He had died from exposure.

Manie was given a pauper's funeral and Monty and Uncle Danny were the only people to attend.

This Christmas my mother was broke as usual, and since we only had a primus stove there was no special lunch — Uncle Danny had given my mother money for take-away fish and chips. Uncle Danny also invited me to his home, asking me not to tell the others. He told me to come up after lunch, at about 4.00 pm, when the family was resting. He told me to knock on the kitchen door at the back of the house. He would be waiting for me, he said.

When I arrived the door was open and he was waiting for me.

He sat me down and served me the plate of food waiting in the warmer. He told me to enjoy it and that when I had finished I should clean the plate and the cutlery and close the door behind me. There were a few different meats, roast potatoes with gravy and loads of vegetables. As I was finishing my lunch I heard a Christmas carol being played on a piano. I washed my plate and cutlery and quietly followed the sound of the music. I did not go far – the room right next to the kitchen was the lounge. I peeped through the open door. Uncle Danny was sitting at the piano, his back to me, and those huge blacksmith fingers and hands were moving lovingly and with gentle dexterity about the keys. I stood transfixed for a while, and then left quietly.

Chapter
Fourteen

'Leslie, get the kettle on, and the pot on the stove for boiling water ... quickly! You, Mario go to Aunty Okkie and get clean towels, as many as you can, not bladdy dirty ones, now hurry!'

Linda was lying on the single bed in a foetal position, groaning in pain.

I was white with fear and in a state of silent, inert panic.

'This poor child, what have you children done? My God, I hope she survives this. You'll have yourselves to blame, if anything happens ... I haven't delivered a baby in years ... and this child is too far advanced for an abortion. You should've all known better!'

My mother was angry, but surprisingly calm. She knew that under the circumstances she was desperately needed to help us.

Linda was close on four months' pregnant and had gone to a back-street abortionist in Woodstock earlier that day. When she got home she was in pain, but the woman had told her to expect that. She should just bear it, and the foetus would pass later that night, she was told. I don't think the woman knew, or cared, how far into her pregnancy Linda was. She was happy for the money, I suppose.

By about 8.00 that night Linda and I both knew she was in serious trouble. Going to a hospital was not an option – abortions were illegal in those days and carried a jail sentence.

I got hold of my ex-brother-in-law, Leslie, who had a car, and asked him to take us to my mother, who had just come off day duty at the Wynberg Medi-Clinic where she was nursing. She was a midwife in her early years of nursing. Having had nine children herself, and four miscarriages, she had plenty of experience.

I fetched the towels and Leslie and Uncle Danny – with whom my mother was living at the time – got the water to boiling point. Then my mother sent Leslie and me from the room. We waited in the next room. Linda's anguish was unbearable.

After a while, I just heard sobbing. My mother came out of the room, her face stern and white, carrying the foetus wrapped in a towel.

'Here's your baby, Mario ... it's a little girl.' The way she uttered those words, no malice, no sarcasm, blew me away. I was too shocked to cry. 'Go and do what you have to do now. Leave Linda here to rest. You can come and fetch her in the morning.'

I thanked my mother. She didn't want any thank you, she said. Leslie and I drove to a green belt close by and buried the baby.

We dug a shallow grave and covered it with earth and grass-stuffed sods.

I heard her crying out. Small life, without voice. Small life, without breath. Crying out ...

It was the darkest moment of my life.

If there is any sin I have committed for which I am prepared to take the ultimate consequence, this is the one. I have never come to terms with it. I doubt I ever will. Everything else I have endured pales in the dark light of this decision.

* * *

Linda was 17. I was barely 22.

We first met at the Constantia Cinema in Wynberg, through my sister Lillian. I was on my first 10-day leave from the Army – I was based at 5SAI in Ladysmith, Natal – having just completed my six weeks' basic training. Linda was 15. She had strawberry-blonde hair and an athletic build; she was an excellent ice-skater, and used to skate, and compete, at the ice rink in Lester Road, Wynberg, close to where I was living with my mother at the time.

I started going out with Linda after completing my military service. I moved into her home, because conditions in mine were appalling. The move didn't improve things much. I slept on the couch at my mother's house. I slept on the couch at Linda's. Linda shared a room with her two younger sisters and her only brother. Her eldest sister lived in a room with her boyfriend. Her mother had her own room. Her sister's boyfriend, John, did not like me much and felt threatened by my presence. He was much older than me. Linda's mother was an alcoholic and drank at least one bottle of brandy a night. So did her sister and her sister's boyfriend. There were rowdy, tearful fights almost every night.

John confronted me one night and told me that the house was too small for the two of us. I ignored him.

Soon Linda fell pregnant. I was still working at the Standard Bank in Plumstead. I had to work for nine months after completing my military service, in lieu of the nine months I had spent in the army, when I had been paid my salary by the Bank, less my small army pay of 50 cents a day.

When Linda was about six months' pregnant we married in the Wynberg Magistrates Court. Her mother and my mother were the only witnesses. The magistrate did not notice that Linda was only 15. I don't think he cared. I remember him smelling of booze.

Linda and I celebrated with a half-jack of cane spirit, and that was that.

We moved into a boarding house room in a big block near Muizenberg Station. There were only communal toilets and bathrooms. By this time I had started as a trainee salesman at Edgars in Parliament Street.

Linda gave birth to our son, Paul, two weeks after her 16th birthday. January 14, 1971. I turned 22 in June of that year.

We were both immature, and fought and bickered a lot. She fell pregnant again soon afterwards – for some reason she had stopped taking her contraceptive pills. That's when she had the abortion. Not a few months after the abortion, she fell pregnant with our second son, Gianni. By the time she was three months pregnant with Gianni, I moved back with my mother. Sleeping on the couch again.

A short while later I met Margaret. That marriage lasted for six years.

I left Margaret too, and met Carla in Johannesburg.

In 1980 Carla and I, Paul and Gianni, were living in Norwood, Johannesburg, when I received a call from Linda. She was in Harare. She had been living with a man there and was three months pregnant. He had left her. Could she come and stay with us for a while, until she found her feet? She had already met Carla, when she originally brought the boys to me in Johannesburg. They got on well together.

Carla, without any hesitation, agreed, even insisted, that Linda come and stay with us. 'For the sake of the boys too,' she said. Those were the years when I was working with Bruce and Helen on Paperchain, the gift and greeting card company.

Linda arrived and settled in quickly.

They were very happy times.

She started work within weeks of her arrival, and between them Linda and Carla did the shopping, cooking and cared for the boys. We had a domestic worker, Sarah, who lived with us. When Linda's baby was due, Bruce, Carla, my friend Carey and I accompanied her to the Marymount Maternity Hospital in Kensington. When the nun on duty came into the visitors' waiting room to inform us that Linda had had a little boy, and to ask who the father was, we all stood up.

Linda was at a loss for a name and it was Bruce and Helen who suggested Kerin. Linda liked the name. Within ten days of Linda's return home, she and I took Kerin by bus to Home Affairs and registered him as Kerin d'Offizi. She had asked me if it would be okay for him to take the same surname as the boys; with no maintenance or alimony strings attached. I agreed completely.

There was absolute harmony in that home for all the time that Linda stayed with us. When Kerin was about 18 months old Linda decided it was time to move on and return to Cape Town, where her family lived. After a year or two, for whatever reason, she stopped contacting the boys. Every Christmas and every birthday, from then until they saw their mother again when we all moved back to Cape Town, Carla would give them extra money, and say, 'Your mom sent this for you.'

Many years later, in 1996, when I part-owned the restaurant in Cape Town, Linda would help make sweets and salads, and do the books for my daughter Gabriella, who was the restaurant manager. The most formidable team in the hot kitchen, especially on Friday and Saturday nights, when we turned over one hundred covers in a fifty-seat restaurant, was that of Paul, Gianni and Kerin.

Chapter
Fifteen

When I arrived home one holiday, this time in Johannesburg, my mother was living in a one-bedroom flat in Hillbrow with 'Uncle' Henry. Lillian and Alba were living with them too. Henry had lost a leg in a motorcycle accident and landed up in the ward of the hospital in Bloemfontein where my mother was nursing at the time. My mother had never qualified as a nurse. She had started in the laundry at this hospital, after my father had left her, and worked her way up to the position of nurse-aid. She should have been a fully qualified nurse. She was such a bright, gentle and compassionate woman.

She nursed Henry for weeks while he recuperated. By the time he was ready to be discharged he and my mother had become very fond of each other. Because he had nowhere to go – his family didn't care much about him – my mother took him in; he still needed a lot of care and attention. He was just over thirty when I met him. My mother was over fifty. They married soon after he left hospital and a short while later moved to Hillbrow.

Even with the loss of his leg Henry was a large man with huge arms and a massive torso. He had a thick crop of wild red hair and an equally thick, red, handle-bar moustache. His arms became even more powerful because, until he had his prosthesis fitted, he relied on crutches. He was seldom without his crutches though, and only wore the prosthesis when he went looking for work, or when he found work, where he generally only stayed for a short while. He was exceptionally bright, well-spoken, and had a wealth of general knowledge, especially about sport. When it came to rugby or cricket he could tell you who played in which position in almost any past game. 'So-and-so played fly-half for the Springboks in 1932 ...' I was fascinated by this; and at the same time sad that such a talented man was in this state – a desperate alcoholic without a career.

At age thirty-one Henry drank brandy, mostly, but really anything he could lay his hands on.

As time went by, he became increasingly violent towards my mother, especially when he was coming off the drink and suffering DTs, as my mother would explain it to me. *Delirium tremens*, the state in which Henry hallucinated, became frustrated, swore, screamed and beat my mother.

'There he goes again, chasing the pink elephants,' she would sigh. They were threatened with eviction many, many times because of the shouting and screaming – especially the screaming from Lillian and Alba. My mother always managed to stave off eviction with promises that things would change for the better. Soon.

Lillian, Alba and I slept in the small lounge, sharing a couch and a single bed between us. I only spent a holiday with them once a year, in August. Lillian and Alba lived with them permanently and saw a lot more than I did.

We called Henry 'peg-leg' and 'hop-along casualty.'

My mother had found work at a hospital in Hillbrow, and Henry was out of work. We were on social welfare, and every Wednesday Lillian, Alba and I would go to the OK Bazaars in Hillbrow and exchange the food coupons my mother received from welfare. We could only get the necessities like bread, milk, sugar, porridge, cans of cheaper fish – like pilchards in tomato sauce – and the odd vegetables.

My mother had a painting of an exotic lady hanging on the lounge wall. I was convinced that it was a saleable piece of art and offered to find a buyer for it. During my wanderings around Hillbrow and the city centre of Johannesburg, I had come across the Johannesburg Art Gallery, at the bottom end of Joubert Park. I took the painting to the art gallery one day. I did not have the money to pay the entrance fee, but I asked the cashier at the entrance if there was anybody important I could speak to, as I had a good painting to sell. I did not know it was a print. An elderly lady approached me and asked me exactly what I wanted to sell. I showed her the picture. On seeing it, without even taking a close look at it, she twisted my ear and escorted me outside, warning me never to repeat this prank and never to set foot in the gallery again unless I paid my entrance fee. I was embarrassed and a little hurt. I returned the painting to my mother. She kept it for many years and I later established that it was a Tretchikoff print – his famous Spanish Lady. My interest in art began with this episode and years later, when I could afford it, I would visit art galleries quite regularly.

One day Henry, dressed smartly in jacket and tie and wearing his peg-leg, asked me to accompany him to town, where he had set up an interview for a job. We took the bus. After his interview we passed a bottle store. He told me to wait outside and went in, buying two half-jacks of brandy. He placed them, each in its brown paper bag, in the two side pockets of his jacket. He told me that he had landed the job. He was starting tomorrow and it was time to celebrate. He had just come off the drink and a few days of the murderous DTs.

I was too young to argue or advise.

Henry had used our return bus fare for the brandy, and now we had to walk the long journey home, from Commissioner Street, up the steep incline of Twist Street into Kotze Street in Hillbrow, where we lived. I was young and fit enough to manage. I did the walk regularly. Before leaving town, we sat on a bench in an open public area in the city and Henry finished almost one bottle before we set off on our walk. He cursed the pain caused by the chafing of his prosthesis as we walked, and the more he complained about the pain the more regularly he would swig large mouthfuls from the brandy bottle. He fell to the ground a few times, when I would try desperately to help him to his feet. On one or two occasions a passer-by would help, but generally people would just walk past. We managed to get home, though it was quite a long while after leaving town.

Henry was meant to start work the next day, but he could not, or did not want to. He was back on the booze. This was the pattern of his life.

* * *

'Dear Mamma, I'm coming home tomorrow, and if you don't mind, could you meet me at the train ... Dear Mama ...'

I hummed the words to the melody of this country song as the train approached Cape Town. I saw Table Mountain for the first time and the top was covered in cloud. It was the August holidays and I was excited at the prospect of meeting my elder brothers Monty and Victor for the first time. My mother had moved with Henry to Cape Town. She had written to me at Boys' Town and told me she was now happy to see all her children regularly. She was pleased to be back in Cape Town, which was where she first married and had her first five children, my brothers David, Wally, Victor, Monty and my sister Eileen. Apart from David, who had since emigrated to Canada, all her children were in Cape Town. Lillian and Alba were still living with her and Uncle Henry. I had not yet met Victor and Monty.

My mother and Henry were in a one-bedroom house in Stranton Road, diagonally opposite Wittebome Station. Stranton Road runs parallel to the train line. It was very noisy when the trains passed by, especially the express trains that didn't stop at the station. The windows of the house would rattle, so close were the moving trains.

I had just turned thirteen. My mother met me at Cape Town Station alone.

The house had a yard that was actually part of the blacksmith's shop right next door. When we arrived at the house I was thrilled to see all the horses and carts in the yard.

Uncle Henry had not changed, although he was sober when I arrived. My mother told me on the train home from Cape Town station that he hardly ever worked these days and that his drinking had become worse. And that he was still '... chasing the pink elephants ...' between heavy drinking binges and drying out.

That evening I met Monty and Victor, who had come to see me. Monty was resplendent in his police uniform, with gun at his side and handcuffs attached to his belt, and Victor was also dressed in a smart nursing uniform. Monty was 21 and Victor 19.

I saw them a few more times during those holidays, and I remember Monty taking me to Newlands rugby stadium to watch Western Province play. Monty was fanatical about rugby, especially his team, Western Province. He was on duty that Saturday afternoon and managed to get me a ticket.

It was a rainy, miserable August and the lounge where Lillian, Alba and I slept was permanently wet. There were massive leaks in the roof and despite the number of buckets and bowls on the floor and on the little dining table to catch the rain, we had to move the single bed and couch into my mother's and Henry's room so that we could sleep, dry and relatively undisturbed.

I would have preferred the rain and the wet.

Henry had a white enamel bowl with a handle – a piss-pot we called it – next to the bed, in which he would spit, piss, crap and even vomit at all hours of the night, especially when he was drunk. Some nights he would start off in a jovial way, joking and smoking while lying in bed with my mother, but when the lights were put off we could hear him tossing about under the blankets bothering her. And we'd hear her hoarse whispers and pleas: 'Leave me Henry, not with the kids ... I've got to be up early for work.' Then we'd hear him curse and swear. We'd hear the sounds of him slapping her followed by her quiet sobbing. Lillian and I, who always shared a bed, would just hug each other tight in the hope that a storm would not break. Alba would climb into the bed with us. Some nights, when he was not drinking, just before the DTs took hold, he would lie in bed smoking and tell me stories about Springbok rugby. Those happy occasions were rare.

One night I was playing around with Alba in the lounge and my mother and Lillian were preparing bacon and eggs in a frying pan on the primus stove in the kitchen. Suddenly Henry screamed for my mother from the bedroom: 'Joyce, where's that brandy? Where'd you hide that fucking brandy!'

My mother shouted to him from the kitchen that she had no brandy, that there was no money for brandy and that he'd better get over it. 'I'm cooking supper for the kids,' she shouted above his cursing and swearing. All of a sudden he came storming from the bedroom on his crutches. He was pretty able on them and only fell when he was completely drunk. He was wearing white underpants and a white vest. The stump of his leg was covered in cloth. He moved quickly past Alba and me into the kitchen. We followed him, Alba screaming at the top of her voice. Once in the kitchen he started demanding brandy from my mother, telling her that she was to find the money and go to a shebeen. She refused and tried to calm him. He lifted a crutch and hit her across the back. Then he threw his weight at her, pushing her against the wall and grabbing her by the throat. By this time she had fallen to the floor and Henry was bent over her.

Alba screamed louder and I began to cry. Lillian was calm. She lifted the pan with boiling oil, bacon and eggs. Turning the pan, she hit him on the back. She did not just hit him. She held the pan to his back for quite a while. He let out a terrible scream and collapsed in a heap next to my mother. He must have passed out with the pain because after that scream, followed by a few grunts and moans, he lay quiet and still for a while. Lillian began to sob and my mother calmed us all down. Later on she managed to get him to bed and treat his burns, which were severe. The next night she brought from work some extra medicines, dressings and bandages for his wounds.

The next day Monty and Victor came to visit. When they heard about what had happened the night before, they dragged Henry from the bed, my mother pleading with them, saying that he had suffered enough, into the little entrance hall and pounded him with their fists and feet. I had never before seen anybody get such a hiding.

I returned to Boys' Town a lot more grown up.

When I came home again the next year Henry was gone and my mother was living with Uncle Danny, in the back room of the same house. She had been evicted from the main house because she could not manage the rent. Henry had beaten my mother once too often. Monty and Victor bought a single ticket to Johannesburg, put Henry on the train and warned him never to return.

We heard years later that Henry had drowned in the Vaal River, south of Johannesburg. The story went that he was on a rowing boat with some friends one Sunday. They were all drinking when the boat capsized. Henry was the only one who drowned. When I heard the news I felt a little sad for him. My memories were not, and are still not, bitter. When I think of Uncle Henry I think most of his incredible knowledge, especially when it came to sport.

Chapter
Sixteen

At first I did not hear the knocking on the door, the music from our portable radio was so loud. Carla, my mother and I were relaxing in flat No 2, Park Lane Mansions. Paul and Gianni were in bed. It was quite late. Carla asked 'Is that a knock on the door?' It wasn't surprising, as we knew most of the people in the block, and many came to visit, or to borrow sugar, coffee, milk, and even marijuana.

We had a little curtain covering the small glass panel on the door. I drew it open a little and saw Frankie Boyum. What was he doing here? I opened the door and was confronted by four or five men with Frankie. They were detectives, and told me that they were looking for my brother, Leandro. I immediately put my arms around Frankie, kissed him on his cheek, and whispered in his ear: 'You're too late, you mother-fucker. Leandro is dead.' Frankie's face whitened. He dropped slowly to his haunches and keeled over. Fainted. He groaned as he fell. One of the detectives bent down to attend to him.

I said to the detectives that my brother, Leandro was dead. I was angry. 'I have my mother from Cape Town with me. She is inside and mourning. Please leave. My brother is dead. He committed suicide. We buried him a few days ago in Cape Town.' They didn't believe me and insisted on coming inside; two had already entered the flat and were in the tiny entrance hall. 'You're going to fucking upset my mother,' I said. 'If you don't fucking believe me, why don't you contact the Diep River Police Station in Cape Town. Please, leave us alone.'

By this time Frankie had come to, and the detective who had been shaking him by the shoulders and lightly slapping his face pulled him to his feet. "I hope I don't ever see you again, Frankie,' I said. Before they left one detective said that they would be back if I was lying. I'd be in deep trouble for harbouring a wanted criminal. They left. My mother had been drinking white wine, was a little pissed, and was unaware of what was happening.

Leandro had committed suicide a few days earlier, and about two days after his funeral, my mother had driven with me and my friend Carey from Cape Town. He was driving. I had suggested that my mother take a break and spend some time with me, Carla and the boys.

I heard, after being told of his death, that Leandro had been involved with a gang of armed robbers who robbed banks in Johannesburg, Pretoria and Durban. They had been doing this for about 18 months when the police caught up with them. Leandro had escaped the police dragnet, and fled to Cape Town. One of the robbers was killed in a shootout with the police. During the same shootout, another had shot and killed himself because he had broken his leg in the escape attempt.

The others, I think there were three of them, were sentenced to lengthy jail sentences. I read the reports in *The Star* newspaper. They had referred to the gang as The Shotgun Gang. Frankie Boyum had turned state's evidence. Since he was Norwegian, he was sent back to Norway, a free man.

At the time of his death Leandro was living with a woman, Iris, with whom I had had a brief affair many years before. Leandro, I heard from my sister Lillian, in whom he had confided about the gang, knew that the police were closing in on him – he had heard from friends and drug dealers that they were making inquiries about him and his whereabouts. One day, after Iris left for work, Leandro drank a bottle of gin and about seventy Vesperax tablets.

My sister Lillian broke the news to me. It was very late at night; Carla and I were returning from Hillbrow. As we passed through the Park Lane Mansions entrance hall we heard the telephone in the public booth ring. It was normal for anybody who lived there to answer the phone. The call was for me. It was Lillian and she was distraught, almost incoherent; she was going on about how Leandro had chosen to die on her birthday, May 25.

I borrowed money from my boss and flew to Cape Town the next day. My father arrived from Natal the next day too and we went to identify Leandro's body at the Salt River morgue. As we were staring at the body through the glass panel my father fell in a heap and begged me to locate his heart tablets in a pocket of his jacket. I found them easily and gave him one with water, brought quickly by an attendant who had been with us when we identified the body.

Then my father composed himself and told me to be strong.

The funeral service was held in a Catholic church in Plumstead, and Father Sham, the priest who was then in charge at Boys' Town, flew down to conduct the service at my father's request. It was a sad service. For once, I was not an altarboy or a choirboy, as I had been at so many funerals before. After Father Sham had said the concluding prayers, and directed us to our hymn books for the farewell hymn, 'Nearer My God To Thee,' which my mother had requested, there was a slight pause. Suddenly, in a gutted voice, my father cried out in broken English, his cry filling the vast space of the church. 'One more kiss for the child … please, please … one more kiss for the child.' He staggered in a daze to the open coffin, kissed Leandro once and draped his head, arms and upper body over the coffin, sobbing uncontrollably. There was a stunned silence.

We buried Leandro in the Plumstead cemetery, a short distance from the church. I stood next to my father at the graveside, watching him closely. He was calmer. After the burial service, when my father, mother, Father Sham and most of the mourners had left, Lillian and I and a few of Leandro's friends sat at the edge of the grave, feet dangling above the coffin, and smoked a few joints. Lillian had insisted we do this. That night we went to a club in town. I don't remember much of the night or the following day, except that I heard and danced to the classic hit 'I Will Survive' for the first time. The song triggers memories of Leandro every time I hear it.

* * *

'… did you read or hear recently about a landmine explosion on the border where it was reported that no one was killed or hurt? Actually, it happened near us on the road that runs past here. Well, it happened to 33 Battalion, consisting of Unita, FNLA, Ovambos, and our troops. They carry AK-47s and wear browns or anything. Man, the corpses have been rolling in here for the SAP. They just fuck into Angolsh to get 'em. Anyway, a white lieutenant was killed when the Mog cartwheeled and another black had shrapnel in the back. The Mog was a wreck like a sardine tin stood upon. Please write if you can, you know what it's like to receive post, especially up here. Keep well and God bless. All my love and kisses to Gaby and it's fucking hot here you know. The rainy season has started and it's just sand and more sand. Lots of love, Leandro … GRENSVEGTER…'

Border fighter. Leandro spent two years in the army, most of it on the Angolan border, and when he returned he was not the sensitive young man I had always known.

He had also spent time at Boys' Town. He was there with me during my last year, and another year after I had left. At fourteen he had somehow convinced my father and Aunt Lolly to let him live with them and go to school on the South Coast. He went to Port Shopctone High, but was expelled two years later. He had been caught in bed with the principal's daughter.

At sixteen, and ever since he was a young boy, Leandro wanted to be an actor. I was married to Margaret at the time and my father asked us if Leandro could board with us while he attended the Maas Philips School of Drama in Cape Town. My father would pay the fees and his board. Until he went to the army, Leandro lived with us most of the time. He did well at Maas Philips and flew through the RADA (Royal Academy of Dramatic Arts) exams with merit.

Before he went to the army, though, Leandro went to Mozambique with a good friend of mine, Paul. Paul was involved with the Students' Representative Council at the University of Cape Town, and was a political and social radical. Like many radicals, he was the son of a pastor. Paul taught me more about the politics of the time than most, except maybe for Father Patrick. Mozambique had just gained independence, and Frelimo was fighting the war against the Portuguese. Paul was going to volunteer his help in the reconstruction of the country. Leandro was going with him.

I will never forget the day Paul came to collect Leandro for the trip, his yellow Volkswagen Beetle loaded to the roof. I didn't see Paul again until after Nelson Mandela's release in the early 1990s, when he returned to the country and I was put in touch with him by a friend in the film business. Pure accident. My friend's name was Jeanne and one day she asked me to invite her to a Sunday lunch; she said we had a mutual friend who was quite keen to see me again. Somehow, in their discussions, my name had been mentioned. She arrived at my home one Sunday soon afterwards – with Paul. He had stayed in exile all these years, and was now returning to help with the reconstruction of South Africa. By this time he was an economist, highly degreed, specialising in minerals and trade.

Leandro missed the 'drugs, sex and rock 'n roll,' as he put it, and left Mozambique after a few months. A short while later he was in the army. After completing his two years, mostly on the border, he came to stay with Margaret and me in Durban. At this time I was restless, unhappy in my marriage, and deciding to leave Margaret. Leandro and I headed by train for Johannesburg, to Park Lane Mansions and Carla.

While Leandro lived with us he worked as an assistant to one of Johannesburg's most talented, colourful and respected photographers (he was also an extremely competent painter), Richard Cutler. Although we were all taking drugs at the time, Leandro went overboard. In the year prior to his death I knew of about twelve friends, casual acquaintances, one or two who lived in the same block, who had died from suicide or overdoses. When Leandro broke up a six-month relationship, the girl committed suicide. This devastated him.

He met another crazy girl later, Annette, who, in a drugged state, also tried to kill herself after a major blow-up with Leandro. She threw herself from the balcony of the third floor of Park Lane Mansions and landed in a bush below, which saved her from more serious injuries; she only broke a leg. We joked that she lived only because she fell into a Yesterday, Today and Tomorrow bush. When Leandro and a friend went to fetch her from the hospital they put her in the back seat and did not close the door properly. The friend and driver, JJ, sped around a circle not far from the hospital. Annette fell out and broke a few ribs. They took her straight back to the hospital.

Marion, our friend from the third floor, told me one day that she was worried about Leandro, and that he was hanging around with heavy guys who were into serious drugs. On more than one occasion I reminded Leandro of a solid little maxim I had always applied to myself: 'Ride your pony, don't let your pony ride you.'

Like all drug addicts he denied the extent of his excesses, giving me the 'I only do it once in a while.' Marion told me of an occasion one Sunday night when Leandro arrived at her flat to visit, along with two of his friends. They were desperate for a fix. There was nothing available, so they liquidised boot polish and injected it into their veins.

For weeks, even a few months at a time, Leandro would be away. Only after his death did I know why. They didn't rob banks because they wanted the money. They needed the drugs.

Sixteen months after Leandro died Carla and I were returning by train from a holiday with my father at his South Coast home. Paul, Gianni and Gabriella were with us. This was 1980, the Paperchain, Bruce and Helen time. We left Durban Station on September 16.

That afternoon and night, until I fell asleep, I couldn't wipe the Kyrie from my mind – the Latin hymn I sang so often as an altarboy, at so many funerals during my youth. Not even the rhythm of the train could drown the constant and continuous incantation of the Kyrie. I cursed out loud to Carla that the hymn would simply not go away. I hadn't heard it for many years.

When we arrived at Johannesburg station we were surprised to see Bruce and Helen waiting to meet us on the platform. We were not expecting them. They broke the news that Lillian had died the night before.

I still have Lillian's death certificate. The cause of her death, according to the certificate, was simply asthma. It wasn't true. My brother Monty visited the room in Muizenberg where she had been staying with a boyfriend, a drug addict. Monty had established from various witnesses that the boyfriend had beaten

Lillian viciously that day and night. He also heard it from the owner of a shop, who said he had seen it happen that afternoon, outside his shop.

When Monty went to have a look at the room where she was staying he found blood smears on two of the walls. Monty used to be a policeman. We trusted his investigation. The boyfriend was arrested, but released after one night because of lack of evidence. His father was the commanding officer at the Muizenberg police station at the time. We heard, six months later, that the boyfriend had hanged himself, somewhere in Midrand, Johannesburg. We buried Lillian in Leandro's grave, as she had always asked us to do.

Years later, when my son Gianni married his schoolgirl sweetheart Tracy, he bought his first home, a flat in Diep River, near Plumstead. He invited Carla, my mother and me to lunch one day.

When we entered the flat, my mother took me by the arm, squeezed me as if holding on for support and said in a soft, but hoarse voice: 'My God, Mario ... Leandro died in this very flat!'

It was all too much for me at the time.

I maintained my composure.

Chapter
Seventeen

Goebbels took us both by the hand – the three of us holding hands – and began to pray. And babble in tongues.

When he stopped, Matt asked him if he could say a prayer. This seemed to please him. And Matt began his performance. He quoted chapters from the bible. He prayed for our souls. This was not the Matt I knew. His nickname amongst his fellow conflict journalists – he had told me sometime back – was Mad Matt.

I didn't know whether to laugh or cry. I started to giggle. Muffled giggles. I wiped my eyes, as if wiping away tears. I felt like a choirboy in church. When one choirboy breaks out into giggles, it becomes a laugh, moving across the group in a wave, until the whole cracks up in loud, uncontained laughter.

At last, Matt stopped praying. Goebbels thanked him, stood up abruptly and said goodnight. I asked him what time we could expect him the next day. He smiled and said, 'I'll be in touch.'

It was approaching midnight. We went to the little toilet and smoked, looking out of the window. I noticed little bonfires burning along the road below. I didn't hear any artillery, I remarked to Matt. He squinted, peering down the road. The bonfires were small piles of rubbish being burnt. There were clearly no refuse trucks collecting rubbish.

Matt pointed out another interesting sight. Below, we could see dozens of dogs and cats scavenging about. During the day there wasn't a dog or cat to be seen. They would have been skinned and eaten, Matt said.

We went back into our room. Back to the bed lice and the mosquitoes and the restlessness. Before falling asleep, we recalled the day – particularly the recent prayer session – and cried a bit with laughter.

Lights out.

I got up at about 3.00 am, checked my watch, went to the toilet. I had a pee, lit a smoke and peered out of the window. The fires were still smouldering.

And then I cried.

I cried for the people of the Congo. Cried for the soldiers, the police. Even the traffic police. Even the immigration officials. I cried for Africa. For myself. For the victims of cyclical wars. War after war after war. Fuck Kabila. Fuck the corrupt dictators, the despots and the warlords. And fuck the West, the East, North, South. Capitalists, Socialists, whoever. Fuck 'em.

We woke early. I heard Danny's voice coming from his room. I got up, left our room, knocked on the door. Rauhu opened. She let me wash my face and fill my water bottles. Neither Matt nor I had washed or bathed since the previous Sunday morning, before leaving Zambia.

Matt joined us. They had a window with a view. The view was washing, hanging from wash lines on the balcony of a dilapidated complex of flats opposite. Matt went to the window. '

Jesus!' he exclaimed, 'come check this, Mario!'

There, on the windowsill (actually the corrugated iron roof of a lean-to, attached to the outer wall), were piles of dirty syringes and needles. And there was other filth and rubbish, used condoms and balls of soiled cotton wool. We were staying in a bona fide drug den.

Matt went to our room to fetch his camera. He took a few shots of the view, some close-ups of the syringes. A little later, he informed me that he had a few francs, and that we might be able to afford a small breakfast at the Metro Babel downstairs. We had enough money for three slices of bread, with butter only, and a cup of black coffee. In the Congo, milk powder costs extra, almost as much as the coffee.

We sat for a long while, sipping our coffee and chatting.

A young man, sitting at the table alongside us, asked us in perfect English where we were from. He knew the church well; often attended their services when he was in Lubumbashe. He told us that he too was a photo-journalist and that he lived and worked in Johannesburg. He was visiting family.

The roller coaster turned up, aiming at the heavens.

We invited him to join us at our table and we chatted a while. He offered us another cup of coffee. We related our experiences so far. He was shocked by the treatment we had endured at the hands of the church. When we discussed the fact that we were only allowed to use our cameras inside the church, and that we would love to shoot in the streets of Lubumbashe, he offered to help. As a Congolese, he said, he had a better chance of filming. Not that it would be easy.

169

But he had connections.

Because the price of videotapes was exorbitant in Lubumbashe, he asked us for a blank tape. He accompanied us to our room. Matt gave him a tape. He and Matt swapped cell numbers, and he promised to contact us in the morning. We mentioned that we hoped to be on our way out of the Congo by mid-morning. He said not to worry, he would be in touch.

By midday, there was no sign of Goebbels.

We spent a few more hours with Danny and Rauha. They told us that their car had been fixed and that they too planned to leave the following morning, on their 5 000 km trip to Windhoek. They'd be driving to Lusaka, where they would proceed to Botswana, across the Caprivi Strip and into Namibia.

Matt and I both made a mental note of their plans. The fact that they were driving to Lusaka pleased us. Maybe we could catch a ride with them if we had problems getting out of the Congo.

The afternoon passed quickly. At 6.00 pm, we were back in our rooms. Goebbels arrived. *'Entrée! Bonjour!* Let's go!' His usual manner. I grabbed the tripods, my rucksack and camera and a Captain Morgan Rum all-weather raincoat with hood, in case it got cold later. Goebbels offered to carry it, slinging it over his shoulder.

We followed him downstairs. This time there was no RTIV green Toyota waiting for us. 'We take public transport tonight,' he said.

We walked a short distance to a taxi rank. Bedlam. We squeezed into the back of a mini-bus and got off at the main church, where the green Toyota was waiting for us. We would be visiting four branches of the Come and See Church tonight, Goebbels explained, to film exteriors and signs, as well as a few interiors, pastors and members of the different congregations. And we would be interviewing both himself and Bishop Lamba Lamba.

We spent over an hour travelling between the four churches. As we stopped at each, Goebbels would direct us impatiently. 'Matt. Take shots of the church. Mario, go inside, shoot the pastors and the congregation.'

While travelling between the churches I saw a KFC chicken outlet with the familiar face of Colonel Saunders emblazoned on the shop front.

It read KATANGA FRIED CHICKEN.

At the last church, Matt stepped out of the car, camera ready. He stepped onto what appeared to be a grass verge. It wasn't. His left foot went knee deep through the grass, into a furrow. He tumbled over onto his side. When he recovered he got back onto both feet and took a few stills of the church. His left leg was covered in shit. He had stepped into a sewer.

We returned to the main church, where we interviewed Goebbels and Bishop Lamba Lamba. Then it was back to the Hotel Babel. Goebbels bade us goodnight, goodbye and wished us a good trip back to Zambia.

We were dumbstruck.

He knew we had no money. We were supposed to have been under the care and protection of his church.

Did he have no heart?

Was he brain dead?

Or was he just a motherfucker with a hidden agenda?

Before we had left the main church earlier we had seen him come out of the bishop's office carrying a large pile of money.

Brand new notes, neatly wrapped in plastic. Not crumpled, soiled notes from the collection baskets.

As he walked away from us and toward the green Toyota parked outside the entrance of Hotel Babel, he turned to me, pointed at my raincoat, still attached to his shoulder, and said, with a glimmer of a smile, 'And this is mine.'

'Please have it, Pastor Jeff,' I replied, 'but it needs a wash.'

It was my favourite all-weather jacket. Black, with a Captain Morgan fishing logo embroidered on it, and warmly lined inside. I always took it up Table Mountain when I hiked. Often, my hiking friends and I would take a few joints to smoke on top of the mountain, or in one of the indigenous forests. Often, I would nip a joint and put it in one of the pockets of the jacket. I prayed there was a nip of a joint in that jacket right now. I prayed that customs would get him when he arrived in South Africa for his upcoming bible conference.

Back in our room, we discussed our options. We had only R700 between us. To go to the Bureau de Change in the morning to convert our money would be dangerous. There would be soldiers and police waiting for us outside. We knew this without any doubt at all.

We had three options. One, walk. Two, catch a ride with Danny and Rauha. Three, maybe the journalist we had met that afternoon would help us make a plan. He seemed a genuine type.

Matt suggested another option. While standing in front of the hotel, or looking down on the road from the toilet window, we often saw dozens of war cripples bumping along the road in little three-wheel box cars, ingeniously made to navigate the pock-marked roads using levers. He suggested we hijack one of these, and taking turns pushing, we could get to the border in a couple of days.

We spent the rest of the night in fear and apprehension, not knowing what tomorrow would bring. We thought about the Immigration Officials who had been questioning Danny about us the day before.

Every footstep along the corridor chilled my blood.

The bed lice attacked relentlessly. Strangely, there were no mosquitoes.

Maybe we smell and would taste too bad for the mosquitoes, Matt joked. Not so funny. We hadn't bathed and now Matt stank even more with the shit clinging to the one leg of his jeans.

Matt gave me a sleeping tablet. It didn't help me through a restless, fearful night.

Up early. Same routine. But this time we smoked freely in our room. There would be no Goebbels today, that was for sure.

At about 8.00 am Matt's phone rang. Sweet music. Our new-found friend, the journalist. He asked how we were. He told Matt that he would be filming some scenes of Lubumbashe and would see us in less than an hour. He was waiting for a friend to give him a lift.

We went downstairs, stood in the warming light of the morning sun, stretched our legs and smoked. Then hell descended – the two Immigration Officials. The same two who had been harassing Danny and Rauha. They beckoned to us to follow them into the foyer of the hotel.

'Passports!' they demanded. My hands shook uncontrollably as they plunged into the eleven different pockets of my jacket. I found my passport in an inside pocket and handed it to one of the officials. Matt handed over his as well. My knees wobbled. My mouth dried up again. Sweat coursed down my forehead and into my eyes. They scrutinised our passports. We noticed that one of the officials was holding and 'reading' one of the passports upside down.

'Problem,' the one said. 'Problem,' the other repeated.

I couldn't handle the suspense. 'Matt, sort this out, I'm going outside, maybe sit in the coffee shop.' I went next door and sat at a table. When a waitress brought me a menu I ignored it. She must have seen the fear in my eyes. She left me alone.

I sat there, dazed and confused.

Then one of the Immigration Officials walked in, pulled up a chair, and demanded 20 dollars. I pleaded poverty. He wouldn't take no for an answer. 'Problem,' he kept on repeating.

I stood up and walked to the open kitchen. I pleaded with Paul, the chef and owner, to help me. On one occasion – the one and only time we had had a decent meal in the establishment – I had complimented him on his cooking. Now he was my only escape. He walked the short distance with me, back to the Immigration official.

'What is the problem?' he asked. I explained that the Immigration Officials had said there were problems with our passports and that they wanted money from us. We did not have any money, I assured him. I begged him to explain to the official that Pastor Jeff had been paying our way. That we were missionaries in the Congo by invitation of Bishop Lamba Lamba.

The official then said that I must phone Pastor Jeff. I told him I had no phone. He told me to use the restaurant's phone. I insisted that I had no money.

Paul spoke at length to the man. Then, thinking quickly, I told Paul to tell him that Pastor Jeff was coming to collect us at about 2.00 pm, and I was certain that the matter would be solved then. The Immigration Official said we were not to go anywhere and that they'd be back.

I thanked Paul and returned to the hotel foyer. Matt was standing there forlornly with the other official. His complexion was whiter than white. One of the officials wagged his finger threateningly at Matt, and in a gruff voice said, 'You finished with Bishop Lamba Lamba, but you not finished with us.' He also told us to stay where we were. They would be back.

The phone rang again. It was our journalist friend. Matt told him we were in deep trouble and please to come to the hotel as soon as he could. Within half an hour he arrived with a colleague. We were waiting for him downstairs. We told him what had transpired and he said, 'Okay, let's go fetch your luggage. We leave now.'

He and his colleague accompanied us to our room. His colleague was holding a video camera, shooting the entire scene. All the way up the stairs and into our room, he had the camera trained on us. Inside the room, he had me in his sights. Our journalist friend told him to put the camera away. He then handed Matt the tape we had given him the day before.

In a voice filled with urgency he said, 'Hide this tape in the bottom of your bag. If they find it and see its contents you'll both be in very serious trouble.' Matt tucked the tape into a pair of socks, which he buried in the bottom of his rucksack.

Our friend then asked, 'please, promise me that when you make your movie, and when you write your stories, you will never, ever mention my name and that I have done this for you. If you do, you will compromise me and my family.' We gave him our word. I looked him in the eyes and said, 'your name is Archangel Michael.' He smiled at me.

We made off down the stairs, to a waiting car outside. On the way out he had a few words with the concierge, indicating his watch. He bundled us into the car – there was another man in the driver's seat – and we sped off through the streets of Lubumbashe to a large taxi rank on the outskirts of the city. When we came to a stop, Michael spoke hurriedly to the others in French. Then they all reached into their pockets for money. The driver was talking on his cell phone. Michael turned in his seat to face Matt and me. 'Now listen carefully,' he said.

He handed me a bundle of notes, Congolese Francs. 'This is money for the taxi that will take you to Kasumbelesa. Put it safe in one pocket.' I handed the bundle to Matt. 'Then,' he added, handing over another bundle, 'These are dollars for Kalouji. We are speaking to him now. He will meet you at the border gates and take you through to Zambia. Give these dollars to him.' These I also I handed to Matt, reminding him to keep the bundles in different pockets.

He handed me a few more notes. 'Mario, if Kalouji has not met you within five minutes of your arrival, use this money, it is 7 000 francs, to phone him. You will find plenty of stalls where they will sell you airtime or phone for you.' I put them in my pocket.

The driver wrote a number down on a little piece of paper. 'This is Kalouji's number,' Michael said. 'Do you both understand?'

We said yes.

'Okay, let's go.'

We climbed out of the car and he led us to a taxi he had singled out. He took me by the shoulders, gripped them hard, looked me in the eyes and said, 'Mario, you and Matt are soldiers of God. You will walk safely, because God is with you. Remember that. God will keep you safe.'

We hugged him in turns. The roller coaster was flung from its tracks.

We sat in the car. The heat coming through the window was searing. The taxi would not move. Not until it was full. I was getting agitated. I squirmed in the seat. Matt gripped my leg, squeezed, and muttered sternly to me, 'Chill, Mario. Chill, brother.'

A fattish lady got into the back seat with us. Soon after, two well-dressed young men climbed into the front. There were six of us in the taxi. I was so relieved I introduced Matt and myself to our fellow passengers. The woman in the back was Lillian. I thought of my sister. The two passengers in front were Paul and Alex. I thought of my son, who would be leaving for New Zealand. I made a mental check of the day and date. Yes, Paul would be flying out tomorrow, June 8.

We sped to the border. We passed a few roadblocks. I felt fear, and a sense of loathing. Each time we were stopped, the driver climbed out, approached the soldiers, signed a form and paid some money. The windows of the car were tinted. It was just as well.

On the way to the border I suddenly remembered the pink crystal Steven Minaar had given me. I asked the driver to slow down a little. I then tossed the crystal through the driver's open window. It landed in the bush on the side of the road.

I had fulfilled my promise.

In under an hour we arrived in the hell called Kasumbelesa. My heartbeat went nuts at the sight of the place. The driver stopped close to the border gate.

By now, I took nothing for granted. I offered Alex, one of our fellow passengers, the francs Michael had given us to call Kalouji. It wasn't necessary, because within minutes a man approached us, and with outstretched hand and a beaming smile introduced himself. Kalouji. 'Quick, let's go,' he urged. Instead of going through the gate a little way ahead of us, he turned to the left, pulling us with him. We wove between shacks and houses and ended in a run-down house that appeared to be a shebeen. There were seven or eight men around a large table, drinking beer and playing cards.

Kalouji pointed to a bench near the entrance and asked us if we would like something to drink. We nodded. 'Give me your passports,' he said, and walked hurriedly out of the back door. A young girl brought us Fanta Orange drinks. They were ice-cold. We drank, relieved.

We waited. Matt mentioned to me later that he had been extremely concerned that Kalouji had taken our passports. One thing you always hold onto when doing this sort of work is your passport. But Kalouji reappeared.

'Quickly,' he said, and motioned us to follow him. I didn't really notice much. But we saw no soldiers and no police. He was taking us through the back door of the border post. Before us was no man's land. Beyond it the Zambian border post.

Just as we thought we were safe we walked into the Intelligence Officers of President Joseph Kabila. The same ones who had greeted us on our arrival, three days earlier. I shuddered when I saw the man with the coloured bandana, the jeans and the dark glasses. He was sitting on his stool.

'Put your bags down,' he commanded. He indicated a spot at his feet. 'Twenty dollars and we no search your bags.'

Nothing matters to a man who says nothing matters. I lost all fear. I held the flaps of my jacket open, as if baring my chest, and shouted, 'Shoot me, you motherfucker. You people have played with my mind, my heart … with everything … just fucking shoot me!'

Kajouli gripped my forearm, squeezed it gently, and quietly said, 'Chill, my brother.' Then he glared at the man with the bandana and sunglasses. It must have been a powerful signal. The man just sat, perched on his stool.

Kalouji helped me with my luggage and we walked across no man's land into Zambia.

I gave Matt my passport. He could sort out the paperwork. I went outside, onto my knees and kissed the soil of Zambia. Not just a kiss. I buried my lips in the soil.

Kalouji waited until our passports had been stamped, then walked us to a taxi. He said farewell and added, 'You are safe now, my brothers.' I thought about the taxi fare and confided to him, 'We don't have any Kwacha.' He smiled his broad smile and said, 'We have taken care of everything.' I took my cap off and placed it on his head. He thanked me. It was a bluish, Cuban-style cap; a Fidel Castro cap. I had worn it throughout my stay in the Congo. Matt said it made me look more like a mercenary than a missionary. When I saw photographs of myself later, I knew I had been stupid.

We climbed into the taxi. The driver said we would leave as soon as the car filled up with passengers.

A young, smartly dressed girl got into the back seat with Matt and me. She didn't stay long. She muttered something under her breath, climbed out and joined the driver in the front. She said a few words to him.

We drove off to the sounds of Reggae music. After we dropped the young lady off, I asked the driver what, if anything, had been wrong with her. Or us.

He laughed. 'She told me that you white men stink.'

Chapter
Eighteen

Like most of us, I had always heard about the power of the owl. As in ' ... he or she is like a wise old owl...' but I had never witnessed or experienced this until Craig's death.

Craig was my nephew, Lillian's son. When Lillian died tragically, Carla and I paid a lot of attention to Craig and his brothers: Wayne, who was the oldest, Gavin, and, much, much later, to his sister, Bronwyn.

It was a Wednesday, early evening, about 5.00 pm, the sun still shining, when my six year old daughter, Mirella – she and I were playing by the swimming pool – suddenly pointed to the roof of our house, and exclaimed: 'Daddy, daddy, look, there's an owl on the roof!' She was ecstatic. I had never seen an owl so close, in daylight. I had heard them before, long before, and at night only. The only owls I'd ever really seen were in cages, or in books, magazines or the movies.

Mirella was so excited, she called Thelma. Thelma was a Xhosa woman who worked for us, and helped bring Mirella up from the age of one. In the classic South African relationship of masters and servants, Thelma was part of the family. She lived in a self-contained flatlet on our property. She was a large, gentle woman, and came outside when Mirella called to her so excitedly. 'Look, Thelly, look up there ... there's an owl!' Mirella pointed to the owl on the roof. By then Carla was outside, standing next to me, also looking at the owl. Thelma looked up, her hand shielding her eyes, and exclaimed: 'Howww! ... Merio.' She looked at me and Carla and said, 'The owl brings bad news, Carla, Merio.' She pronounced my name like that, with an *e*. 'Howww!' she repeated.

I half-laughed and said. 'In your culture, Thelly, maybe, but the owl in mine is a wise creature.'

She told me that in her culture, in Xhosa tradition and lore, the owl was a harbinger of bad news and death. And so it was, for us too, that night.

Just after 11.00 pm my nephew Wayne, Craig's elder brother, phoned to tell me that he had located Craig, after two days of searching for him, at the Salt River Police morgue. He had been killed on the M3 early on Monday morning, on his way to work. His front tyre burst and he hit the Woodstock turn-off sign and was killed instantly. He had his identity document on him, and a telephone booklet with numbers of his friends and family, but nobody contacted any of us and we waited out those anxious days.

It was my daughter, Gabriella, who had alerted us to Craig's absence on the

Tuesday night. Gabriella and Craig had become very close and were sharing a flat in Gardens, close to Cape Town's city centre. Carla and I had recently sent both of them to Italy, Gabriella to my family in Palestrina, about 50 km east of Rome; Craig, to Milan, to see if he could break into the international modelling scene. He was an incredibly good-looking boy, with blonde hair, blue eyes and an athletic build. He was one helluva fighter too – he grew up in children's homes from a very young age. Craig had seen a lot of life.

On the Sunday before, we had what we referred to as a 'Granny weekend.' My mother, whom my children and their friends called Can Gran – because she loved her semi-sweet white wine and drank copious amounts of it – was very ill, and had been staying with Carla and me for a while. Carla and I really thought that Can Gran would die soon. She was 79. We brought the family together for what we believed would be our last 'Granny weekend.' Craig came to the lunch, where we were quite a few. They were always very happy, sometimes raucous, these lunches. They often went on late into the evening. But this one was more sombre; there was a sadness amongst us. Can Gran was very frail and had no more than a couple of glasses of wine that she sipped very slowly. She retired very early, way before sunset.

Craig had arrived on his motorbike, a recent purchase. He pointed out that the front wheel was a little wobbly, and that he would sort it out during the week. When he left after the lunch, we all told him to get home safely.

Gabriella told us that Craig did not come home on the Monday night. She thought little of it because he had quite a few girlfriends. She thought he was probably spending the night with one of them. By Tuesday night she had not heard from him – that's when she phoned me, and Craig's brother, Wayne. We phoned friends of his, then hospitals and police stations; to no avail.

In desperation, Wayne went to the Salt River Police Morgue, and found his body.

It was 1995. Craig was just 25 years old. We held his funeral service in the little stone chapel in the grounds of the Marsh Memorial Home in Rondebosch, where he had spent most of his early years, before going on to Teen Centre, also a home for underprivileged and / or problem children. After Lillian died we occasionally brought Craig and his brothers to Johannesburg for school holidays, and, on leaving school, he spent almost three years with Carla and me and our children. He and his brothers were our other sons.

We spread Craig's ashes on his mother's grave; the same grave in which my brother Leandro was buried. The shock of Craig's death proved to be a sort of elixir for Can Gran, and she recovered miraculously. She died two years later, at 81, from a sudden stroke. She outlived four husbands and a few of her children and grandchildren.

A few weeks before Can Gran died, Carla and I invited her and her boyfriend, Bill, twenty years her junior, to come and live in the cottage Thelma had stayed in. Thelma, too, was ill and went back home to live with her family in the Transkei.

I always teased Can Gran about her 'toy-boys.' Bill was just the last of them. She always smiled and said, 'Remember, the factory might be closed, but the playground's still open.'

We spread her ashes, as she had requested, on the grave of Leandro, Lillian and Craig. We toasted 'Can Gran' and the others; we had brought a bottle or two of wine for this occasion. I remember an eerie feeling coming over me. I remarked to Carla: 'This gravesite is getting like 'Crowded House.'

Alba was with us, and she remarked that she too would like her ashes placed here one day when she died. Four years later, before her 48th birthday, she too died tragically. We spread her ashes on 'Crowded House,' as requested.

As I write now, it's early November of 2006. This Sunday past, October 29, I was having drinks with Carla's brother Ray, at my local, Mambo's, in Plumstead, a walk away from my home. The manager, Matthew, a good friend to Carla and me, asked if he could speak to me, in private. We went to a quiet spot and sat alone at a table. When Matthew had first started work at Mambos, just before Christmas, we all liked him immediately. That Christmas Eve, before closing early, Matthew told us a little forlornly that his folks were abroad and that he would be spending Christmas alone. Carla and I invited him to spend the day with us. When Paul left for New Zealand, a few years later, Matthew adopted me as his 'other' father. He told everybody in the pub that I was his adopted dad, and he my adopted son.

He was feeling down and told me that he was a failure. He wanted to talk to me in absolute confidence. Nobody but his parents and family knew of his past.

'What do you mean, a failure, Matthew? You're a success, incredible at what you do and extremely popular.'

He answered the question by telling me about his past. How he'd run away from home at age twelve to join the circus. Which he actually did, for a while, becoming a fully-trained trapeze artist. 'There you go,' I said, 'You're not a failure.' He insisted he was, and told me that he had been sent to a place of safety and then on to Teen Centre, where Wayne and Craig had been.

I said nothing, just told him that I too had been to children's homes – like Boys' Town, I said – and that there was nothing to be ashamed of. I did not feel like a failure simply because of my past. 'Tell me more about Teen Centre,' I asked. His face lit a little and he told me about some of the times and some of his friends. He told me about his room-mate. A boy a little older than he was, who protected him and who taught him to fight.

'I remember bringing a hi-fi player when I arrived there, and this guy was happy because he loved his music ... he had pictures of models all over the fucking walls of the room!'

'Was his name Craig Brown?' I asked, incredulously.

'Where do you know Craig from? Yes, his name was Craig Brown ...You knew Craig?'

I had known Matthew for all of four years, and only now I was hearing this. Matthew became very excited. 'How's Craig, where is Craig?'

I told him Craig had died a few years ago.

He stared at me; tears began to stream down his face. I felt a few coming on too.

He took my hand, squeezed it very tight, and repeated, 'Now I know why I called you my adopted dad ... now I know why I adopted you as my other dad.'

I called out to Ray, sitting a little way away at the bar. Ray approached us. Before he sat down I said, 'Ray, tell young Matthew here about Craig Brown.'

Very dramatically – as is often his nature – Ray cupped his hands around his lips and imitating the sound of an owl, and stretching the syllable O, said: 'The Ooowl,' and added, 'He was my nephew too, Craig Brown.' He looked at us both quizzically and noticed the tears, which by now Matthew did not even bother to hide or wipe away.

Matthew said: 'Now you're my adopted Uncle too, Ray.' Ray is a tough nut – a builder and tradesman, who had dived up the rugged west coast of Southern Africa for many years. On hearing what had just transpired he sat there with us, tears unashamedly streaming.

We told Matthew the story about the owl. We told him other stories too. He insisted on hearing all, because, now, he said, he was really part of the family.

We phoned Carla to join us.

We drank beer and shooters late into the night.

It seemed like the right thing to do.

Chapter Nineteen

'I am torn between two masters, the shepherd and the wolf; between two mountains, in a valley that is green.'

This is how I summed up and described my duality, my extremism, to my shrink. He had asked me to articulate or write down what was bothering me at the time. I always liked to think that I could pull off a comfortable balancing act and centre myself, despite my extremes or the pressures from the shepherd and the wolf. But I was seeing the shrink because the valley was not, in fact, that green. I was actually in a rocky place – my life was becoming more arid by the day, despite the fact that I was co-creative director of an extremely successful advertising agency in Cape Town, and the directors were throwing money at me.

I always travelled to work by train, and still do. On my way to work each day of the week, every damn day, I would encounter street kids and beggars. I became friendly with one beggar in particular, Danny, who used to sit on a bench in St. George's Mall. Danny was blind. He lived in the northern suburbs, in a back room with family. They used to drop him at the station each day, from where he would take a train to Cape Town and find his spot in St. George's Mall. I often bought coffee or a cool drink for both of us and sat with him for a while. We'd chat and joke, sip our drinks together. He had a great sense of humour. When he was robbed going home, particularly on Friday evenings, he would tell me on the Monday morning that he had been 'robbed blind.' And chuckle.

One morning, about 11.00 am, while sitting at my desk, for no reason I could understand, I started sweating, palpitating, hyperventilating. The skin on my wrists and neck reddened and itched, and a strange, incredibly uncomfortable heat filled my body. I left the office and the building and went to my favourite coffee shop, Emgees, in St. George's Mall, a short walk away. I drank four beers in less than a half an hour and calmed down almost immediately. I grabbed a few mints after settling my bill and went back to the office. Since the beer had helped, I was not too worried about what had happened. Maybe it was a once-off.

But it happened again a few days later, and then more frequently – every few days.

Drinking in such a short time at such odd hours was not the answer. So I went to my doctor. I was having panic attacks, he explained. The last time I had experienced anything like this was when I was 21. I was now 45. The doctor referred me to a shrink.

I was also having very powerful and disturbing dreams.

I was also living a lie in advertising.

I was also having reckless fun, late lunches, parties all night.

I was also neglecting myself and my family. The hours were crazy and you never knew what would happen next. Late nights, weekend work, all-nighters, deadlines, deadlines, deadlines. It was all part of the rush.

Blind Danny and the street kids had gotten to me. I told the shrink it was obscene that I could be earning so much money while others starved or begged in the streets. He told me that what I was feeling and experiencing was typical behaviour and that he had come across many cases like mine. He knew of a case where a man had committed suicide because of his social guilt. He tried to help me rationalise my feelings.

The dreams persisted. He urged me to write down one particular dream. I didn't need to. It was so vivid, so real, I remember it with all-consuming clarity.

I remember sitting at a very large wooden desk, being interviewed for a job by a beautiful, green-eyed blonde, the head of an ad agency looking for a writer to handle a new account. She struck me as a tough bitch; the introduction was sterile and almost unfriendly. I suddenly stood up and walked across the room to study a large picture hanging on the wall to the right of me. I stood before the picture, 4 x 3 metres in size at least, a sort of collage of maps and other obscure pictures and little portraits mounted in an impressive frame.

I was completely – and unintentionally – ignoring her.

I turned to look at her. She was smiling. 'Do you like that picture?'

'I think it's interesting.'

'If you go down the passage, right at the end is a little room, you can't miss it, just open and enter and you'll see a few more interesting pictures.' Her smile beamed at me now, softened by a touch of glee. Her humour redeemed her in my eyes.

I nodded and opened the door to the little room at the end of the passage. I felt queasy as I stepped in.

There were two large portraits hanging about a metre apart on the wall facing me as I opened the door. On the adjoining wall, I noticed one other. I took them all in, in one swift glance. The one on the right was a portrait of Christopher Columbus. A dark, stern portrait of the man who had discovered the Americas: arms crossed, hands clasping his shoulders, a frightening scowl – almost a growl – on his face. He was set against an embattled background of smoke and fire, ships and dismembered sailors.

I could faintly hear the screams of the sailors and the terrifying din of cannons.

I wanted to see whether the painting had been done in oils or acrylics. I stepped within touching distance of the portrait, when, out of nowhere, Christopher Columbus threw a backhand that brushed my cheek. Startled, I stepped back – a very large step – and stared at him in horror; his face now red and blazing with anger. I remember exclaiming and calling him a 'fucking arsehole' as I moved across to the other picture, keeping my eyes on him, not taking any chances.

The portrait hanging alongside was bright and cheery, with vibrant, yet soft and calm colours: pinks, whites, creams, blended with subtle touches of greens and blues. It was of Liberace, the pianist. Dripping with jewels, as usual. And with a warm, smiling face. I could hear the light tinkling of piano keys and a melody softly resonating around me.

I was hesitant to take a closer look. Then, from where I stood, I clearly saw him wink at me. He winked again.

I muttered to myself, 'Some people never change,' and turned to face the adjacent wall. There hung a picture of Elvis Presley.

Thinking, '... now, Elvis ... that's a really cool guy!' I instantly – and unafraid for some reason – stepped right up to the picture to touch it. It was mounted behind glass. I looked closer and saw that it was a print. Like a Hollywood movie poster. Elvis didn't move.

Columbus tried to slap me and Liberace winked provocatively at me. It must have been because the picture was a print and not an original. I was disappointed. Intrigued. Confused. I was also relieved that Columbus' backhand hadn't connected. I stepped backwards through the door, closing it quietly behind me.

I never saw the blonde again. Interview over.

When I awoke from the dream, I was confused, yet calm. Intrigued, yet content; as though there were a mighty revelation awaiting me.

I got out of bed. The usual ablutions. Work.

It was only a few days later at the office, during an important presentation to a major client, that I began to reflect on the dream. The interview. The blonde. The three portraits. Why was Elvis, the only print, expressionless?

And then I decided.

Listening to all the bullshit being thrown around the room, egos bursting at their already inflated, stretched-to-the limit-seams, I concluded that the Elvis symbolised plastic. Hollywood. Shit. And that the others were real. The portrait of Elvis was just a lifeless, cheap print.

The dream repeated itself, over and over again. Fast-forward. Rewind. Forward, back.

I thought about the contrasts.

The blood and guts of conquest, war, destruction, agony and mayhem surrounding Columbus, however violent and disturbing, were, despite all the horrors, real and human. The same went for the softness of music, poetry and art, however effeminate the aura of Liberace. He too was real. Gentle, slightly sexy, even sweetly decadent. Elvis – he just didn't perform his old magic, trapped as he was.

The shrink said that the two mountains probably symbolised breasts. Dead right, I thought, and reminded myself that I had probably been weaned too young. I also recalled a thought that I had once put to paper: '... I suckle at the tits of life and even if the milk goes sour from time to time, I suckle on ...' The shepherd and the wolf represented right and wrong, good, bad, light, night, the conformist and the non-conformist, he said. Polarity; duality. He used other jargon to explain it.

The dream, he suggested, was telling me something of great importance and that I should listen to what it had demonstrated. It was my latent, increasingly frustrated need to do what I believed I should be doing, and should have done, all these years.

But I knew that.

I needed to do and write the real stuff. Advertising, no matter how you look at it, is transient, fickle. Devastatingly powerful, yes, especially in the wrong hands. But it paid the bills and suited my nature – living on some sort of edge.

Soon after these discussions with the shrink – I did most of the talking; he took notes and prescribed drugs – I was approached by a friend who asked me to join him and a few others to establish the Cape Town branch of a Johannesburg Black Empowerment agency. Without hesitation I resigned my job and dropped my gross salary by a good few thousand rands. I was restless and my quest for happiness and peace of mind were becoming a priority.

Nothing changed. Different tent, same circus.

With a lot more fun, admittedly . One night at some media party or other I re-acquainted myself with a former colleague. He remembered the cannelloni and lasagne I had made by hand for his house-warming party a few years back, and asked why I did not open an Italian restaurant. Because, he said, he and his friends were still raving about the food. 'And aren't you tired of advertising by now?'

'Its one of my dreams, to open a restaurant.'

'Well, why don't you do it?'

'Don't have the capital.'

'And if you and I form a partnership, and I finance it, would you do it?'

'Of course,' I admitted, a doubting Thomas. People say a lot of things. Make a lot of promises. All the time.

So many people, including my children, had always remarked that making pasta was what I should be doing. It really was a dream of mine. One day, I always promised myself, when I have the money and when I get advertising out of my blood. My friend was offering me the opportunity, right then. We began to talk about the idea. Gianni, my son, to whom I had taught the skills I had learnt from my father and family in Italy, had left a clerical position at the Deeds Office and was now working as a trainee chef at an Italian restaurant. My daughter Gabriella was waitressing. When I discussed the offer with them they said, 'Go for it dad! It's what you've always wanted to do.' Both said that they would support me in the enterprise. I asked them to come along for the ride; to realise the dream. There was no question, they said.

And so we put the plan into action.

It was agreed amongst us that Gianni and our financial partner would look for a suitable venue. My son Paul, working with me as an art director, reminded us all that one needed to study the *Karma Sutra* for clues as to where to open a restaurant. Like the *Karma Sutra*, he said, retail is all about ' ... position, position, position. ...'

Meanwhile, there were exciting prospects on the horizon at my agency.

We had devised a July-holiday promotion around the famous American all-black basketball team, the Harlem Globetrotters. They had been signed up to come over to South Africa and perform in major centres around the country, sponsored by our client, and to make promotional appearances at our client's outlets. They would be arriving at the end of June, a few days before the promotion broke. And we needed to start producing material yesterday. We needed shots of the basketball stars for posters, entry forms and other promotional material, including endorsements for radio spots. The only way to execute the campaign in time was to go to America to the home of the Harlem Globetrotters, in Hartford, near New York. South Africa had become a democracy and Nelson Mandela, Madiba, was president. The timing was perfect. A few years earlier they wouldn't even have considered the offer.

It was the highlight of my advertising career.

I went with my MD and the marketing director of the client company, a suit from the client's above thc-line agency and a woman from the sponsorship agency which had originally signed up the Harlem Globetrotters. We stayed at the Manhattan Sheraton Hotel, off 5th Avenue. During our week in New York we travelled one morning to Hartford where I worked the afternoon recording sound-bites and directed a photo shoot with a photographer we had brought along from New York. That night we watched the Harlem Globetrotters play. Apart from that one 'working' afternoon, it was all party – restaurants and nightclubs. We went to a three-storey club – a converted cathedral – and met some of the strangest people. The first floor was for straights, the second for gays and the third ... well ... They said it was best to stick to the first and second floors.

My colleagues went on countless tours to famous landmarks. I walked the streets or took cabs to little Italy, Chinatown and Greenwich Village. I had seen the landmarks on postcards and in magazines and movies. Now I wanted to feel them.

Every night we ate at a different restaurant. One night we ate at a famous Italian restaurant that seated hundreds of people. You couldn't order a pasta dish for one. You had to order a large bowl that served two. I heard from the lady with us, who had been to New York often, that the Mafia owned the place; it was so smooth, so genuinely Italian. The pasta was unbelievably good.

On the day after we arrived in New York one of my colleagues met up with his brother, who had been living in America for the past year or two. At about eleven that morning my colleague, his brother and I found a tiny bar, patronised almost exclusively by African Americans. A tall, beautiful bar lady from Barbados served us. We asked her discreetly where we could buy good marijuana and cocaine. At first she said she did not know. We hung around, drank scotch and chatted to her. After our third request, she asked if we were FBI. I showed her my passport and my return ticket to Cape Town, and offered to leave them with her until after the deal was done. She said it was not necessary, that we must pay half up-front, and to collect the stuff at 4.00 pm. We went to a restaurant in Greenwich Village, and returned by 4.00 pm. We had bought enough to last us the week. And the week flew. There were times when I wanted to dump my ticket and get lost in New York. On the morning of the day we left it snowed heavily.

When we arrived at Jan Smuts airport I phoned Carla. She told me excitedly that Gianni and my would-be restaurant partner had found the perfect venue, that I would love it – it was a historical thatched cottage with a massive parking lot – and that they had arranged for me to see it on the following day, Sunday. It was in Plumstead, near where we lived.

I liked the place. On the Monday morning I resigned. I was going to fulfil a dream and become a restaurateur.

The writing could wait.

Chapter Twenty

Like most South Africans I was shattered when the news broke about the assassination of Chris Hani on Easter Saturday, April 10, 1993. I watched the television news intently and read every newspaper. It was a sad day for the country. There were jitters amongst many people, whites mostly, that civil war would or could ensue, especially since the assassin was believed to be a member of the extreme Afrikaner rightwing organisation, the AWB.

On Monday morning, April 19, on my way to work, I bought a camera, a little Olympus, fully automatic, with a zoom lens. I had used a similar camera to take pictures at the wedding of one of my best friends, Brandon Platt. The camera belonged to Brandon's best man. The best man was to be included in some of the wedding photos and so he asked me to take pictures for him. Brandon had also hired a professional photographer to record the wedding on stills and video, but chose to mount and frame one of my shots. He and his wife, Lynn, complimented me on that photograph. I was proud of this, and inspired to buy a camera and try my hand at photography.

I had been given a free spool of film with the purchase of the camera and planned to walk around during my lunch hour and take pictures of anything or anybody I found interesting. Cape Town is a colourful, fascinating place with a striking contrast of people: buskers, street kids, *'bergies'* and the rest. At this time I was working for an advertising agency as a co-creative director. Our major account was a large petroleum company. At my previous agency I had also worked on a big petroleum brand, a British-based company. On Nelson Mandela's release in 1990 the agency was briefed to write a full-page ad about how this petroleum company had always supported him in spirit and how proud and happy they were about his now being a free man, taking his rightful place in South African politics after all these years.

Being the only senior writer in the agency, I was briefed. I protested. For the first time in my career I refused to write the ad – on moral grounds. I believed that this particular company did not give a shit whether Nelson Mandela was in jail or not. The managing director understood, he said. A junior writer was appointed to the job.

At about 11.00 am that Monday morning, Maria announced over the intercom that there was huge trouble brewing in town. A protest march had begun and word was spreading like wildfire amongst businesses all over town that serious rioting looked imminent. The office would be closed. We were advised to get home safely. To leave town as soon as we could.

Half-day, we thought, and rejoiced a little.

I walked down the road to the Golden Acre Shopping Centre, through which I would pass on my way to the station to catch a train home. As I approached Adderley Street, across which was the entrance to the Golden Acre, I saw a couple of armoured cars leading a heaving procession of marching, toyi-toying protestors and khaki-clad marshals with horse-hide whips on the fringes of the crowd. The marshals were there, ostensibly, to control the crowd.

Instinctively I started taking pictures. I moved alongside the marchers, keeping a safe distance. I walked ahead of the crowd to the Parade, where the bulk of protestors had gathered, and where I thought they would be addressed by one leader or another. Instead, the rioting began. In the ensuing chaos I shakily snapped away. I took shots of looters and injured policemen and people. I took shots of a burning delivery motorcycle: a long shot, a medium shot and an extreme close-up. I took shots of a post office van that had just been set alight. Three shots of this van. One, smoke billowing from the bonnet. Two, flames shooting forth. Three, the van enveloped in fire. I took a scary shot of a looter as he stood before a broken window. He was smiling at me, a sort of ' .... who's the boss now?' smile. I initially kept close to groups of policemen. But when an assortment of missiles rained down on them – and me, because I was standing with them – I thought it safer to join the crowd.

Which was a little safer, for a while. When my film was finished I searched frenetically in the area close by for a chemist or photographic shop, to buy another spool. Every shop in the immediate vicinity was closed. The adrenalin had so overcome me I felt no fear, or at least not enough to make me quit and go home. I was recording a momentous incident in our history. I felt I had to see it through.

I had to walk quite a long way to find an open chemist, where I bought another spool of film. I returned to the Parade, where I headed straight into the crowd. At one stage a few men started throwing bits of brick and concrete at me. An elderly woman came to my assistance by shouting loudly at them: 'Los hom, hy's van die pers,' ('Leave him, he's from the press'). I didn't have any authorisation or press identity. It was the last thing on my mind. In the prevailing chaos it did not really matter to anyone.

The mood deepened, the looting and plunder increased, the fires were started in dirt bins and vehicles and in and around shopfronts. The whole area became engulfed in smoke. The police started using teargas and rubber bullets. I did what everyone else did. I fell to the ground, eyes watering and burning from the teargas. I was momentarily blinded. I lay prostrate, protecting my head with my hands. I held onto my camera.

I heard people screaming, shouting, cursing. The sounds of gunfire. Running footsteps. Then the firing stopped. When I was able to see again I got up and hurried, half running, to a group of policemen standing alongside an armoured car. I had two or three photographs left in the camera, and as I moved warily to the station, across Strand Street, I took the last shots of the group of policemen. There was a look of resignation on a few of their faces, and behind them, a desolate scene of smoke and little burning fires. One of the policemen had a swathe of white bandage about his head. The white of the bandage was reddening.

When I got home, breathless with excitement, the adrenalin still pumping throughout me, I told Carla about my ordeal. She was really angry. She told me I had been very stupid and irresponsible. In a way, I thought so too.

That same evening, Monday, April 19, I watched a replay of the funeral service that had taken place in Johannesburg. The ceremony was being conducted by Catholic priests. I didn't know that Chris Hani was Catholic. The main priest officiating at the funeral mass was Bishop Reginald Orsmond, now the Bishop of Johannesburg. Father Orsmond.

The next day, Tuesday, I left on a midday flight to Johannesburg for a two-day radio recording that had been pre-booked the previous week. Before my flight I took my film to Tothills, a photographic store around the corner from the agency. I collected the prints on my return. Some of the shots were blurred — I had been shaking with fear a lot of the time. When friends and colleagues saw the photographs they urged me to send them off to the newspapers.

But by then, of course, they were old news.

Chapter
Twenty One

'Silent Night, Holy Night,all is calm, all is bright ... round young Virgin Mother and Child ...'

The melody of the carol resonated through the open windows, lifted up to the fourteenth floor where I was – and upward, to the heavens, I think, carried on the wings of a deep and powerful tenor voice.

I walked to the window and looked out and down onto the courtyard. It had just rained heavily, one of those sudden, voluminous Durban summer downpours. Before I saw the man, the lone singer, I noticed a mist-like steam rising up from the ground. A few people from the same block of flats were leaning out of their windows, dropping coins down to the old man, like steely snowflakes. He was singing with his head tilted back, his eyes to the sky and his hands reaching heavenwards. I recognised him. He was one of the Zulu 'flat boys' – as many men were called in those days. Flat boys cleaned up, served as caretakers and lived on the premises in single servant's quarters. He wore the trademark Zulu sandals, made from rubber tyres, long shorts that just covered his knees and a white short-sleeved, collarless tunic. It was Christmas Eve.

Margaret was on duty, nursing at Addington Hospital, Durban's largest, opposite our block of flats. Gabriella, not even three years old, was fast asleep. I had recently joined Margaret in Durban after our second separation of a few months. We were giving our marriage yet another chance.

Van Morrison, Jim Morrison, marijuana and Margaret – the times of my life filled with abundance and abandon. The early- to mid-seventies.

I met Margaret in a nightclub in Cape Town one weekday night. She was sitting at a table with a girlfriend. I was alone. After a while, noticing that they were on their own – no boyfriends or husbands about – I asked if I could join them. Margaret was the more attractive of the two. Although our eyes met and even locked occasionally, I directed most of my attention and what charms I had at her friend. I calculated that I had a better chance with the friend. Margaret, I thought, was far too beautiful for the likes of me. I established that they were nurses from the Mowbray Maternity Hospital and were off duty, having a quiet night on their own.

It was early evening and there was a live band playing some ambient jazz. I recognised the drummer. His name was Dave and he had been at Boys' Town with me. He joined us for a drink during one of the breaks. When I met Carla, a few years later, she had just come out of a relationship with a guy whose name was Dave. He was a drummer. It was the same Dave.

Margaret and her friend couldn't stay late. Before they left, I gave my work phone number and address to Margaret's friend, telling her that if she felt like it, and if she ever came to Wynberg – where I was managing a clothing store – I would be happy to buy her a cup of coffee. A few days later, just before closing time, a Vespa scooter pulled up outside the clothing shop. Margaret. She parked the scooter on the pavement right by the shop doors. She strode confidently into the shop, greeted me with a wide smile and asked to look at some shirts and ties. I was surprised; taken aback.

While showing her a selection of shirts and matching ties I asked after her friend. She told me that her friend had a boyfriend and would probably not be visiting me. I asked Margaret if she had a boyfriend. She said no, and asked me why I had not given her my details. I nervously confessed that I had thought I never stood a chance with her, she being so beautiful. She told me that she hadn't really come to buy a shirt and tie, but to visit me. 'I'm locking up shop now can we maybe get a drink somewhere?' I asked. 'It's such a lovely afternoon, why don't we go to Clifton Beach and watch a sunset,' she replied. She was carrying a duffel bag. Inside were a bottle of brandy and a bottle of Coke. 'You carry this,' she said, 'And don't drop it.' I climbed onto the back of the scooter with her, placed one had around her waist and held onto her bag with the other.

She was a superb driver and wove her way through the traffic on the highway, through town and to Clifton's 4th beach. At times, on corners, she had the scooter almost touching the tar. I had to be really careful not to break the bottles. I hung on to her, at times holding my breath, closing my eyes. Helmets were not compulsory back then, though she wore one.

She had long auburn-brown hair, pale blue eyes and a statuesque figure. The year before, 1971, she had been crowned Miss Natal and was a Miss South Africa princess. In those days, the 'queens' of the different provinces competed for the Miss South Africa crown. But Margaret was too wild to have become Miss South Africa.

Within weeks we leased an apartment together. Paul was eighteen months old and Gianni had just been born. They were living with Linda, who was living with her family in Wynberg. I was still married to Linda. When Gianni turned three months old I sued for divorce and was awarded temporary custody of the boys. I remember the magistrate asking me: 'How do you presume to ask this court for custody of two minors, the youngest of whom is only a few months old?'

'Your Honour,' I replied, 'I have a home, a job, a family and a permanent maid to look after the children. I can do everything a mother can do, except, of course, breastfeed.' I added that Linda herself did not breastfeed the boys, so it made no difference. Either way, she was going to let me have the boys – we were in amicable agreement.

Margaret had agreed to take on the boys with me, and she came to love them as her own. When Margaret and I married a short while later we took the boys with us on our honeymoon. We spent time with her family in Durban and with my dad on the South Coast of Natal.

We had a Volkswagen Kombi, fitted out with bunks, double-bed, fridge and stove. We also had Van Morrison's 'Tupelo Honey,' 'Domino' and 'Woodstock' tracks, apart from many others. We had other musical fuel for the journey. We had clouds of marijuana smoke. We had the smell of incense filling the kombi for most of the journey. Our relationship was a whirlwind, a wonderland of love, pleasure and fun.

Nearly two years later Gabriella was born. But by this time I was restless again, and reckless. I had a few casual affairs. Then one day, when Gabriella was just three months old, Margaret went back to work, nursing this time at a private clinic. There she met a young man, they began an affair, fell in love and moved, very suddenly, to Johannesburg.

I was shattered. Unfairly so, because I had been unfaithful myself, and until she returned, disillusioned, a few months later, I indulged in a mad, never-ending spree of parties, bedding different women every second night of the week. It was a crazy, drug-induced period of total abandon; of self-destruction. Linda had married again, and she and her husband took care of the boys. This time it was I who could not cope.

After Margaret returned we both vowed to patch things up and stay together 'forever and ever.' It didn't work. I left her after returning from my four-month stint in Angola and she returned to Durban. We tried to patch up our marriage months later in Durban, but again, it did not work.

During more than one Christmas in the years that followed, Carla, Margaret, Linda, my children and I, and various other members of the family would sit down happily to Christmas lunch.

Chapter
Twenty Two

He was tall, muscular, though wiry, and had a few gold-capped teeth. He was deeply tanned. His hair was what they call 'kroes' – short and tightly curled – and a few people said, never to his face, that he was part-coloured; which was pretty normal in Cape Town. There was a thin line dividing whites and coloureds at the time. We lived in neighbourhoods adjacent to each other, and in mixed suburbs, unlike black people, who lived in townships far away from the city yet close enough to commute to work.

Hennie became my best friend, partly because when I met him he was going out with Lillian. I was sixteen when we met and he was in his early twenties. I knew that he had spent his youth in the Constantia School for Boys in Tokai, and that he had recently spent a short time in Pollsmoor prison for assault with the intention to do grievous bodily harm. But in my mind, none of that ever counted against him. He cared for Lillian and he cared for me and protected me. 'Anybody gives you shit, just tell me and I'll sort them out.'

Hennie was exceptionally generous, too. When he bought himself jeans and shirts and other clothes, he'd buy me exactly the same items – same colours, same style. He worked as a bouncer at the Pearly Shells, a nightclub on the main road in Wynberg. Pearly Shells must have been a concert hall in its early days – it was a large, cavernous hall with a stage, where live bands used to perform. One of the famous groups of the time was Jimmy Retief and the Idiots. One Saturday night a large group of national conscripts from the military base up the road gatecrashed the club. They wore civilian clothes. They beat up the band members, cutting off their hair on stage. The band all sported long hair – it was the middle of the sixties. The soldiers were jealous or angry at the contrast with their military-style crew cuts. A lot of them had girlfriends and sisters who frequented the club. The club became chaotic. Hennie and his fellow bouncers, Sydney and Lofty, had their hands full. But Hennie, Sydney and Lofty generally did not come off second best.

Every suburb or region had its strong men. There were the Woodstock boys, the Muizenberg and Fish Hoek boys, the Brooklyn boys and many others. When somebody gained a reputation as unbeatable in a fight, the challenges would pour in. Fights were conducted on a 'gentleman's' basis. No knives, no weapons and no seconds or friends to help. It was stand up as a man, face your opponent and fight. The winner was given due respect and invariably would be challenged by someone else. It was rare that anyone hung on to the title for more than a couple of years – if that.

A few years later there was a legendary fighter in Cape Town itself, Bertie Steyn.

At the same time there was also a very well-known fighter in Johannesburg whom people believed was impossible to beat. He was a Yugoslavian and his name was George the King. The King was an underground figure and some swore he was a hit man. When The King heard about Bertie Steyn, and Bertie Steyn about The King, jeers and insults were carried between the two via the grapevine. Eventually one challenged the other – nobody was sure who – and George The King drove all the way to Cape Town to settle matters. They met one Saturday afternoon on the steps of the City Hall, opposite the Parade. After a lengthy battle Bertie Steyn emerged the winner. That's how it was in those days of ducktails and street fighters.

Sidney, Hennie's fellow-bouncer at the time, used to be the main man in Wynberg; a powerful ox of a man in his late twenties. Sidney's fists had been declared 'dangerous weapons' by a magistrate after countless charges of assault had been laid against him, but Hennie took him down one day. Sidney had beaten Hennie a few times before, but Hennie wasn't one to give up. When the fight took place, the odds were stacked against Hennie. He was a lot lighter than Sidney and there was nobody around who could – or wanted to – take on Sidney, though there were many who tried after Hennie.

Sidney had also been out with my sister Lillian, before Hennie. Lillian was a 'belle' of Wynberg. She had magnificent green eyes and tawny hair to her shoulders. Many a fight happened over Lillian. I never paid entrance into the Pearly Shells, because Hennie would always let me in free, telling the owner I was his younger brother.

And somehow there was a little truth in that. He even called my mother 'mom.'

One afternoon a group of us went camping at Zeekoevlei, next to Muizenberg. We took tents and meat to cook and lots of beer, wine and brandy. That evening we sat around a little campfire we'd made, drinking, talking and playing music. Somebody rolled a large joint and passed it around the circle of friends. Hennie was sitting to my right. The guy next to me passed me the joint.

I had never smoked before. I took it from him and as I placed it to my lips to take a drag Hennie grabbed it from me and gave me a slap across the head. He grabbed the guy who had passed me the joint, lifted him up and head-banged him, following with a punch that sounded like a branch snapping. 'Don't you ever fucking give a *laaitjie* dagga again!'

Turning to me, he warned me: 'If I ever catch you smoking this shit again you'll be sorry that you ever did. You don't want to grow up like this fucking bunch of losers.' He proceeded to smoke the joint, before passing it around the circle. I was bewildered by what had happened. It was his way of showing genuine concern. A few of the guys with us had spent time with him either in school or in jail. He didn't want me to go the same way.

One night I was standing with Hennie in the foyer of the Pearly Shells. A group of four or five guys came in. They were very aggressive. Hennie was alone on duty. I could sense a fight coming and braced myself. I was not a fighter, but if it came to the point where I could help Hennie as back-up, for the sake of my honour alone I was prepared for it. I stood close to Hennie. He put his hand to his mouth, took out his dentures, handed them to me. 'Look after these ...' he said, and tore in. It was all over very quickly.

A year or so later Hennie was sentenced to a lengthy jail term for killing his stepfather.

His stepfather had beaten his mother badly, and Hennie took revenge. He was found guilty of 3rd degree murder. I did not see him again for many years, although at first he used to write to me often from prison; always telling me to make a success of my life and to beware of falling into the wrong company, or getting on the wrong side of the law.

When I did see Hennie again I was living in Johannesburg. He had just been released from Sonderwater Prison after serving over fifteen years. Somehow he had managed to get hold of my mother in Cape Town, who gave him my phone number. He asked if he could visit, and stayed on for a few weeks. Then he left to return to Cape Town. I didn't see him again for at least another ten years.

I also returned to Cape Town. One evening I was driving with a friend along Wale Street, opposite the Cape Town Government Gardens, when I saw Hennie, duffel bag over his shoulder, crossing the road. We were at a standstill in the traffic and I watched him walk up Government Avenue and through the Gardens. I wanted to get out of the car and chase after him.

The lights went green and we moved.

Two weeks later I read a front page article in one of the Cape Town dailies about a crew of workers who had been blown up and killed in the hold of a ship in Cape Town Harbour. The ship was in the dry dock and the crew was doing repairs, part of which required welding. There was, it was reported, a gas leak in the hold and when the welding began there was a tremendous explosion. The explosion blew a massive hole in the ship and killed all ten of the crew.

The next day my brother Victor phoned me to ask if I had heard about the ship that had blown up in the harbour. 'Strangely,' I said, 'yes.'

He told me that Hennie was the foreman of the crew.

Victor and I attended his funeral. It was a small gathering where I saw a few faces from our past. I regretted then that I had not taken the trouble to get out of the car to greet Hennie the afternoon I saw him walk up Government Avenue, on his way somewhere.

Chapter
Twenty Three

Father Orsmond explained to me one day the role Boys' Town was performing in my life, and in the lives of most of the other boys. He said that Boys' Town was my surrogate parent. 'So does that mean you are my other father, and that the nuns are my other mothers?' I asked. 'In a manner of speaking, yes,' he replied, 'In that we are committed to bringing you up in an environment of love and care, and of course discipline and all that goes with it. You are our responsibility while you are here, and as responsible parents we have to put your well-being first.'

I understood the reasoning, but I stubbornly rejected it. I had just returned from the August holidays in Cape Town. I hated the conditions under which my mother was living and struggling, always slogging and battling to survive and support my sisters. Suffering abuse at the hands of Uncle Henry, after suffering abuse at the hands of my father. I had asked Father Orsmond if I could leave Boys' Town at the end of that year, although I would have only a Standard Eight certificate. I told him that I felt I needed to go out and work to help support my mother and sisters.

It was unthinkable, he said, explaining that no parent would consent to this request and that, in any case, I would be doing myself no favours, an inadequate education would be a severe disadvantage, he told me. I told him I did not care. And that I cared even less about logic or norms. I insisted that I could make something of my life. I would become a poet and writer and did not need much of an education for that.

I gave in. 'Yes Father, as you say.' I added, 'Thank you for being my surrogate father, but nobody, nobody in the world could or will ever take my mother's place.'

'And why is your mother so different to your father? You accept the one and reject the other. It's not logical Dof.'

'I don't believe in logic, Father.'

The nuns, however caring they were, could never be my surrogate mothers and nobody would ever replace my mother, no matter what, I insisted.

'So where is your mother at the moment?' he asked facetiously, knowing full well where she was.

'It's not her fault!' I shot back. 'If she had the means, and things had been better for her, I'd be with her now.'

'Why do you always resist the truth and the obvious facts?' he demanded.

'Because they're not my truths,' I replied feebly. He was a master at debate and I could never match him. He always said that I would never end a debate until I had had the last word. 'But ...' I'd say. 'See, there you go again,' he would trick me. He told me that I was typical of the 'arty types,' as he put it. He also said, 'All you arty types should be gathered together and put onto an island far away from normal society, so we can get on with our own devices.'

There was no way I would be released from Boys' Town. My father would never allow it either. At this time I was fresh from a holiday with my mother and was still hurting at the thought of how she was struggling in Cape Town. I was pining for her.

I had a very special relationship with my mother. Most people call their mothers 'mother,' 'mom' or 'mum'; I called mine Momsky. From the age of about thirteen onwards I read a lot of books about the Russian Revolution, and books by Russian writers, translations of course. The characters and writers often had the Slavic 'sky' at the ends of their names. Like Trotsky. Many of the families, especially the children, with whom I identified, were going through hell in their lives: poverty, alcoholism, abuse.

So it was Momsky for me. Most days during my holidays I would walk Momsky to work, and I would be waiting for her after work to walk her back home.

My biggest fear was that she would become a hobo. I saw lots of hobos and bag ladies in the places where I stayed. People living out of broken cars, or languishing on park benches.

My other fear for her was that she would die of stomach cancer; she always complained about pain in the stomach. One night she asked me to go to Joe's Café on the main road to buy some De Witt's Antacid powder. I did not quite get it right, or hear her correctly, and returned home with ant poison. Apart from the rats, there were lots of ants about.

'Are you kids trying to kill me?' she laughed. From then on I got to know De Witt's Antacid. When the pain was so bad she could not move, and when she asked for it, I used to mix it with water for her. Momsky worked in the Wynberg Medi-Clinic until her early seventies, when the matron urged her to leave. The doctors told her that she was more ill than most of the patients. They operated on her – the clinic carried the costs – and she had half her stomach removed.

After recovering she tried to re-apply for her post but was politely discouraged by the matron, who told her she had worked enough in her life. She swore that she could have nursed until the end of her days.

Almost every time I returned from a holiday with her, I would beg Father Orsmond to release me from Boys' Town, so that I could get a job and look after her. And every time he would put his foot down. 'Unthinkable. Never.' he would insist. And, after a week or two, I'd settle into the routine of Boys' Town, school and sport. Until the next holiday.

To this day I thank Father Orsmond for this. As it was I spent four years getting a matric. But at least I had a matric.

The only other person in my life who came close to being a mother to me was Lady Ina Oppenheimer. She would first teach me about things she wanted me to apply, and then set me tasks.

'Today, Dof,' she said out of the blue, before her guests arrived, 'You are going to arrange the guest seating.' Then she told me always to separate partners, husbands and wives. She gave me a list of names and I set about the task. 'Remember Dof, place partners as far from each other as you can. That way conversation will be stimulated. A lot of people tend not to socialise.'

Lady O's farm manager, Mr. Patterson, and his wife, often joined the lunches, with their two daughters. The daughters were about my age, both very pretty, and both had long, wispy strawberry-red hair. That particular lunch I placed the two of them on either side of me. Lady O noticed this and remarked, with a little smile, that I was very smart. She approved wholeheartedly.

She would teach me about the types of wine served with the different meats and meals, and the sorts of cheeses that ought to follow. Often when I arrived she'd say 'Talk to the chef and find out what she's preparing today ... then I would like you to choose the wines for lunch, and remember to ...'

One afternoon, after lunch, I sat with her in her study and she showed me some of her black and white photographs, mostly of animals. She loved animals. One of my favourite pictures was a photograph of a Koala she had taken at London Zoo. I was seated beside her on a sofa looking at the pictures when she suddenly asked me what I thought about her guests that day. I shyly replied that I thought they were all very nice people.

'Don't be shy, Dof, speak your mind. Was there anyone in particular you did not like or you'd like to comment on?'

'I think the tall man with the grey hair who was talking so much during lunch, and who was drinking the red wine, was a bit rude at times.'

'Exactly,' she said, adding, 'I think he is an arrogant twit, so full of himself. But his wife is very quiet and dear.'

We both laughed. She put me completely at ease. From then on I knew that she wanted me to be open and free with my opinions. She always told me to think for myself and never to be afraid to voice my thoughts. Stand up for your beliefs, she always encouraged me. She also told me how she used to collect money for Boys' Town from her rich friends and the wealthy directors of some of the Anglo American companies. She used the terms 'emotional and social blackmail' to explain her method.

She would make an appointment to see a person to discuss a business matter. And of course they would be very honoured, she told me. She would then explain the work being done at Boys' Town and politely ask for a donation. 'They would write out a cheque immediately,' she said. 'But if it was an amount less than I knew they could afford, I would hand it back, stand up to leave and ask, "Is this how much you value the life of a boy?" Always they would apologise and immediately issue another.'

'And where does the blackmail come in?' I asked her.

'Well,' she replied, 'They knew that if they didn't increase the amount they would never be invited to another Oppenheimer function. I would make sure of that.'

I loved her attitude.

At times – when she wanted to rest – she'd give permission for me to row the little boat across the water of the man made lake, to the small island where her late husband, Sir Ernest Oppenheimer, had had his study. She told me where to find the key to the room. I'd go there and relax, feeling as privileged as a king, surrounded by majestic pictures, antiques, rows of books and other personal paraphernalia.

One day, before lunch, we were drinking cocktails in a large entertainment area annexed to the main house. I noticed a picture of Lady O seated with a group of children surrounding her – seated behind her, beside her and at her feet. It was of her and the boys of Nazareth House in Kimberley. I was one of the boys sitting at her feet.

Lady O owned one of the first Land Rovers I had ever seen. It was customised for her with a turret-type hole in the roof on which she could mount her cameras, and from where she could safely take her pictures during trips to game reserves and nature parks. Her driver was a quiet, smallish, elderly man, Mr. Rose.

Not too long after leaving Boys' Town, while managing Swannees in Cape Town, I read a newspaper report about Lady Oppenheimer's death. She and Mr. Rose had been killed in an accident. I don't remember the details. I read that Mr. Rose had died instantly, and that Lady O passed away a few days later. I was incredibly sad about this.

I later heard that she had left Blue Bird Farm, as well as her prize cattle, vehicles and everything on the farm, to her farm manager, Mr. Patterson, and his family. I spoke to Father Orsmond some time later and he confirmed this. He told me that he knew about parts of her will, because she had confided in him on many personal issues, and that she had told him to whom she was leaving the farm.

'The Oppenheimers have enough,' she told Father Orsmond when he had asked her why.

I was extremely proud of her. The will seemed to underline the sincerity, care and compassion she had shown while she was alive. She also left Boys' Town a tidy sum.

The contrast between my mother and Lady Oppenheimer, with her wealth, refinement and status, was enormous. But despite our close relationship, her mentoring of me, the faith she had in me, all her lessons and encouragement, I was still happy that Momsky was my mother. Lady Oppenheimer was the Fairy Godmother who fired my dreams. She taught me never to measure others in terms of their status and wealth, because by doing so, she said, I would diminish my own self-worth.

My mother, though, was possibly the most colourful and kindest person I have ever known; and as she aged she became a lot more colourful. She married four times and outlived all her husbands. All of them, apart from Uncle Danny, who was technically her common-law husband, and with whom she had lived the

210

longest, had been alcoholics. She never touched a drink during her first three marriages and only started a while after she met Uncle Danny.

My mother also outlived two of her children, Lillian and Leandro, a grand-nephew and a grand-niece.

She drank semi-sweet white wine, but if there was no wine, she would drink anything else. She was never an alcoholic and worked until her early seventies. But she did enjoy her wine! She lived in Wynberg for most of her time in Cape Town, and at first my children called her Granny Wine-berg, before progressing to Can Gran, which stuck with her until the day she died. She liked her two- or five-litre cans of wine, depending on what she could afford.

After Uncle Danny died, she had a succession of 'toy-boys,' all much younger than she was. Her last love was Uncle Bill, a tall ex-seaman from Southampton in the U.K. He was twenty years her junior.

Although Carla loved Can Gran as much as we all did, she often told me that she was angry at the fact that Can Gran had had so many children 'nine of us' and that we had all landed up in foster homes or children's homes. 'Why did she carry on breeding if she could not care for you all?' Carla always complained. I would defend Can Gran to Carla, explaining the circumstances of her upbringing. But Carla would not hear it. 'Its no excuse, besides she should've stopped having babies,' Carla would reply.

I personally felt no anger towards her, although there is lot of truth in Carla's words.

After leaving school I was determined to find out all I could about my mother's childhood and upbringing. I taped hours of our conversations, but sadly lost the tapes during one of my many moves from house to house, or marriage to marriage.

Soon after her grandmother died of Blackwater fever, my mother was sent to the Laanglaagte orphanage in the Transvaal, now Gauteng, just a little south of Johannesburg. Her elder brothers, Eric, Paddy and Arthur were at the orphanage with her for a short while. Since I had lost the tapes of our conversations, I have never been able to establish where they had been at the time of her parents' deaths. They could have been living with their uncles in Kitwe (two of her mother's brothers were living in Kitwe, in what is now called Zambia, on the copper belt).

My mother's memory was also sketchy about many details. She told me that when she turned sixteen, after her brothers had long since left the orphanage, they came to visit her one day – after visiting time – and 'they smuggled me into a car and we drove to Cape Town,' she told me. 'I was so happy to get out of that bladdy place,' she said. 'Once a year at Christmas we had hard-boiled eggs ... they were so hard we used to bounce them like tennis balls against the walls.'

After arriving in Cape Town she found work as an au pair for a parliamentary couple. It was in the Government Gardens where she met her first husband, David Hemmings. He was with his best friend, Tommy Greenwood. She was strolling through the Gardens pushing a pram with a child in it, and cradling another in her arms. David Hemmings and Tommy Greenwood stopped to talk to her. She laughed when she told me that David Hemmings had been smoking a pipe and the toddler in her arms reached out and took it from his mouth. She always bemoaned the fact that she married David Hemmings and not Tommy Greenwood. 'Tommy was the gentleman of the two, and had I married him I could have still been with him ... he's still alive and I would have had a better life ... and no bladdy hidings all the time.'

In the last years of Can Gran's life she came to stay with us for at least two weekends of each month. Carla would fetch her on the Friday afternoon and drop her back home on Sunday night. These weekends became known as Granny-Weekends, and all my children and their partners and friends used to come for Sunday lunch. They all loved Can Gran because she was so young at heart, so tolerant and understanding. She was never one for pious platitudes, was never prescriptive, and her actions outshone her words.

The wine would flow and Can Gran would drink most of us under the table. I threw an 80th birthday party for her and we gathered as many family members as were available for the occasion. Never before had she been with so many of her children, grandchildren and great-grandchildren. She said it was the very first birthday party she had ever had. That statement, that truth – she mentioned it quietly, unemotionally – hurt me deeply.

A few weeks after her 81st birthday, she had a sudden stroke and was taken to Victoria Hospital in Wynberg. Coincidentally, my brother Wally's nephew-by-marriage was the doctor who attended to her. Wally had phoned him to ask for special care.

Can Gran could not speak and we communicated with her through touch. She was perfectly conscious though, which made the whole business sadder. One evening a few of us (my brother Victor, his wife Jean, my children and Wayne, my nephew) gathered around her bed and held hands and prayed. We stood about afterwards a, little morose, knowing the end was near. She was on a drip. When a nurse came into the room my son Gianni asked the nurse what the solution in the drip was. She told him that it was medication and nutrients. 'That's not good enough,' said Gianni, 'You are going to have to add some semi-sweet wine.' Can Gran smiled a little smile. She hadn't smiled before during her stay in hospital, and did not again, because she died two or three nights later.

My brother Victor was with her to the very end. I was sorry that I had not been with her too. When we spread her ashes on Crowded House we drank white wine in her memory and toasted her life. I thought to myself that Can Gran would never need to do penance for her sins ... she had already done it over and over during her often miserable and hellish existence on this planet. No God would punish a soul like her. Only weeks before Can Gran died she and Bill were going to come and live permanently in the cottage on my property. Carla had rendered it spick and span and we had planted a rose outside the door, which we named Joyce.

After spreading her ashes Carla and I went to the local nursery and bought another rose, a pink rose, which we planted outside our bedroom.

I named this rose 'Re-Joyce.'

Chapter
Twenty Four

When we arrived in Chililabombwe we asked the driver to take us to a bank where we could convert the last of our money – R700 – into Kwacha.

The bus would leave for Lusaka at 7.00 am the next morning.

It was 3.40 pm when we arrived at the Standard Charter bank. It was closed. Our hearts sank together. We climbed out of the taxi anyway. And then, through the glass windows of the bank, we saw a man. I banged on the window. Loudly. The man opened the doors and greeted us on the pavement outside.

'What is the problem?' he asked, politely. We told him our story.

He listened intently, said he would do his best, asked for either of our passports – Matt handed him his – and he went back inside. A few minutes later he returned with a young lady. On the pavement outside, under the watchful eyes of an old soldier in khaki uniform, he exchanged our rands for Kwacha.

Thursday, June 8.

The first thing I thought about when I woke up was that Paul would be leaving for New Zealand today. 'Goodbye, my boy,' I whispered out loud.

We arrived at the bus terminus before 7.00 am, bought our tickets, boarded the bus, chose seats near the back and settled down comfortably. 7.00 ... 7.30 ... 8.00 ... The bus refused to leave. I went to find the conductor. He told me that the driver was sick. They had sent for another, who would be travelling by taxi from Kitwe.

The bus finally left just after 10.00 am. It broke down twice.

The journey had its funny moments. And a few frightening ones.

We were speeding to Lusaka when the luggage compartment, located on the exterior of the bus, opened and we heard what sounded like glass smashing on tar. The bus stopped. Somebody's ceramic double kitchen sink had fallen out and now lay strewn in pieces on the tar. The compartment was secured, and we continued.

Later, an Immigration Official, wearing a uniform very similar to those worn in the Congo, climbed aboard the bus and began checking identification documents and passports. He looked at ours. 'There is a problem,' he said. Matt and I both protested. He looked again, flipped through the pages, and then apologised for the mistake.

Behind us, in the last row of seats, were a few businessmen, dressed in suits and ties. They were complaining about all the stoppages. One of them said aloud, 'There must be a witch on the bus.' He called to one of his companions and suggested, 'Brother, why don't you go to sleep and dream. Maybe when you awake you can tell us who the witch is.' Matt began quoting verses from the Bible, just loud enough for them to hear.

We arrived in Lusaka after 8.00 pm. The journey had taken 11 hours. We had had only one single smoke break.

After paying for our lodgings the night before, and for the taxi to the bus terminus and the bus trip itself, we had just enough Kwacha to get us to the Eureka Campsite, but not enough to pay for the accommodation. Matt tried to use his credit card at one or two ATMs, with no luck. We decided to go to Eureka anyway. Somehow we would make a plan. On arrival we entered the boma with its quaint little bar and comfortable lounge. The barmen-cum-managers, John and Eric, recognised us from the week before and greeted us warmly. We told them about our lack of money and that we would get to a bank in the morning and settle the bill before we left.

They called the owner. We agreed that Matt would go alone to the bank. We offered our passports and air tickets as security. She agreed.

A young South African, Paul, noticed our tired state and offered us a beer. We ordered a steak roll and chips for supper, and after just two more beers I went to the room in the dormitory, where we had spent our first night, and slept like a baby.

We awakened to a beautiful Zambian sunrise. I felt refreshed. And free.

Matt had left early for town with Paul, the man who had bought us a beer the previous night and who had offered Matt a lift to the bank. I showered and walked about the camp, camera in hand. Shots for the scrapbook. I suddenly felt a little apprehensive. Would we make it to the airport on time? My son-in-law, Ole, would be at the airport to meet us. We would be spending the night in Johannesburg with my family – Ole, daughter Gabriella and their two-year-old son, Rourke. I was longing to see them again.

Matt arrived back from town around 11.00 am. All's fine, he assured me. Karen had deposited enough money for the accommodation and taxi fare to the airport. Not taking anything for granted, Matt had arranged for a taxi to collect us at 1.00 pm. We only needed to check in for our flight at 3.00 pm.

While strolling about the camp, we came upon two South Africans, Julian and Steph, sitting in the sun beside their camper, a 4x4 kitted out with bed, fridge, microwave and stove. They were on their way to Cairo, and from there to the UK. Julian was a nature conservation officer who had been retrenched, and they were emigrating. They offered us cold South African beer – Castle – and Steph made us a ham and tomato sandwich each. I hardly chewed mine, it went straight down.

And then, against the law of averages, and contrary to everything we had recently experienced, the taxi arrived ten minutes early. I hugged the driver and gave him my Ray Ban sun glasses. 'I'm always on time,' he said.

As we approached Lusaka airport I noticed a large billboard with the slogan: SUCCEED THE RIGHT WAY. NOT THE CORRUPT WAY.

We parked. Unloaded our bags. Bade the good driver goodbye, and entered the airport building.

Before passing through customs, we had to validate our tickets at the departure ticket office. And the roller-coaster plunged. The cashier informed us that we needed to pay a departure tax of $20 each! Matt protested vehemently, stating that South African Airways had confirmed that the tax had been included in the ticket price.

The cashier directed Matt to the South African Airways office. He stormed off. I stayed where I was, my heart thumping in my shoes. I looked around at the few people sitting on plastic chairs and milling about. I was preparing to hold a jumble sale: camera, tripod, watch.

Matt returned from the SAA offices. Nobody there. Door locked. He kicked in anger, on principle. I told him that I would sell the cameras. 'Not a fuck,' he said. He would think of something ...

And then Matt showed his genius. Or his Irish luck. He found Karen's Woolworths Visa card in his wallet and took it to the cashier. She checked his passport and noticed the discrepancy in their names. Karen had a different surname.

Matt explained that he had power of attorney. She accepted the card. We were cleared through customs and went into the departure lounge. We drank tap water, with ice. Those around us were sipping at cold refreshments. A beer would have been just fine.

Our flight took off without delay. When drinks and snacks were served, I ordered an Amstel beer and a double Bell's whisky, ice and water. I had another two beers before we landed in Johannesburg, twenty minutes ahead of schedule.

I awoke at Gabriella's house with a feeling of apprehension. And a hangover. I had been so used to everything going wrong, I was ready to get to the train station a few hours before departure, just in case.

We drove almost an hour through heavy Johannesburg Saturday morning traffic to the station, arriving well before the time.

I hugged and kissed my family goodbye. They promised that, on any future trips, we could stop over with them. Gabriella gave me a few hundred rands for food, drinks and smokes. Matt and I walked onto the platform to the waiting train. The Trans-Karoo.

We checked the notice board to see the number of our carriage and compartment. Matt had booked us in as Mr & Mrs d'Offizi so we could be alone for the journey. The conductor greeted us strangely, his clipboard dangling from his hands. *'Môre lieflings!'* he said in Afrikaans. 'Morning loveys!'

We had equipped ourselves with two litres of coke, a dozen beers and a half-jack of Smirnoff vodka. After a few drinks we reverted to army days and sang loudly together.

'Somcone's dying, my Lord, gumba ya ... someone's dying my Lord ...'

The song was truer than we knew.

We had supper in the dining carriage. I had hake and chips. Matt had steak.

We were woken at 6.00 am by the conductor for coffee and a breakfast call. *'Môre lieflings!'* he bellowed.

We wolfed down our breakfast, returned to our compartment and began outlining the movie we would make and the stories we would write. We brainstormed a little. I asked Matt for an appraisal on my performance as a budding photojournalist.

He simply said, 'You got your stripes. I'll take you into a fist fight any day.' Then he apologised for my horror induction into photojournalism. He admitted that most novices are weaned in semi-exotic locations to acclimatise them to different cultures and conditions. Mine, he admitted, was a trip to hell. 'Sorry,' he said.

'No,' I replied. And truly, I was grateful for the journey. It had opened something in me. Had all gone well, we would have had a good church story and an average travelogue about Central Africa. Now we had far more interesting and exciting stuff. And I had undergone the most powerful experience of my life.

The train came to a stop at Prince Albert, a small town in the Karoo. After half an hour the train was still standing. We noticed conductors and other passengers idling about on the platform. We got off the train and asked about the delay.

An elderly man had had a heart attack. He was unconscious. An ambulance was arriving from Laingsburg. It would be here in about an hour and a half.

The ambulance arrived, but the man had died in the interim. According to the law, I was informed, a body cannot be removed from the place of death without a police investigation. The police would be called. They would also have to come from Laingsburg. Another hour and a half. A man standing on the platform began to moan and curse.

'Excuse me,' I said to him. 'This is Africa. The sun comes up and the sun goes down. Nothing, nothing at all, is guaranteed.'

Matt and I climbed back onto the train.

Standing in the corridor, about three compartments from ours, was an elderly lady. She was tiny. She had white grey hair She was wearing a long black dress with a maroon jacket and was speaking animatedly to another lady standing next to her. They were discussing the death of the man on the train. She had tears in her eyes.

Matt and I both mentioned to her and her companion that it was very strange and tragic. She spoke to us in a combination of English and beautiful Afrikaans. She lifted her hands above her head and lilted, 'God has taken one of his sons

219

today, in our company. If God would save us all on this beautiful Sunday, we will remember this day forever. Praise God, praise God.' Then she broke into song.

'You raise me up to stand on mountains,
You raise me up to walk on stormy seas ...'

She cupped her face in her hands and moved into her compartment. We asked if we could join her. She sang more hymns. She cried a little. So did I. We sang along.

We chatted. It made her joyous and emotional when I told her, for some reason, that I had been born in Bloemfontein. 'Bloemfontein? My God!' she exclaimed, in Afrikaans, 'I was married there. Those were the days when weddings were feasts. At my wedding fourteen sheep were slaughtered! All you get at a wedding these days is finger food!'

She told us that she had nursed in Zimbabwe for many years, looking after orphans. She mentioned that every single Monday for the last twenty or so years since she had left Zimbabwe, a prayer group in her former community prayed for her. Just as she, and her prayer group at her present home in Kleinmond, prayed for them.

Every Monday afternoon, without fail.

Her name was Lena. Her husband was with her; a quiet, reserved man. Bernard.

Before Lena and Bernard disembarked at Worcester, she gave us her telephone number and address. Her husband and she operated a guest cottage at her home, and she invited us to come and stay, any time we wished. Matt and I then phoned Karen and Carla to tell them about the delay.

By the time we reached Bellville, the last stop before Cape Town, perhaps twenty minutes from our destination, we had run out of cigarettes. Matt asked the conductor for two cigarettes. He gave us two, and said not to worry about paying for them.

I was home for Carla's 50th birthday, as promised.

We were broke. No money for a big dinner. We went to our local, Mambos Caribbean Bar and Restaurant, in Plumstead, and celebrated with a few Tequilas,

Jaegermeisters and some beer.

The next day, my birthday, June 13, I spent mostly in bed, chilling out, reading and writing a little.

At 5.00 pm, I went along to Mambos to celebrate my birthday with some of our friends. Carla would meet me after work.

At about 6.00 pm, a friend, another Karen, entered the pub carrying a wooden box. She walked up to me, wished me happy birthday, and, handing the box to me, said, 'This is for you, for your birthday. I can't think of any body else more deserving of it than you.'

I was completely taken aback. We hadn't known Karen for long. Before I left for the Congo she had told me that she had lived in the capital, Kinshasa, for close on ten years and that she and her family had been evacuated in September 1991 after the launch of yet another civil war. I had also told her about the pink crystal my friend and colleague, Steven Minaar, had given me to bury in the DR Congo.

I opened the box. Inside were 40 little compartments, made up of simple strips of light wood, and in each, nestling in cotton wool, was a different stone. Beneath each fluffy lump of cotton wool there was a crumpled piece of thin white paper bearing the name of the stone. Beautiful crystals and minerals. Kaolin. Dolomite. Bornite. Calcite Rose. Crystal Quartz. Others I have never seen or heard of. On the rim of each compartment was a little white sticker, numbered in red ink, 1 to 40.

On the inside of the lid of the box was a map of Africa, coloured in with pink crayon.

The hand-written heading read:

ECHANTILLON ... MINERALOGIQUE.

On either side of the map, from 1 to 40, was the description of each stone, with the province in the Congo from which it had originated. And, at the bottom, the words: FAIT A LUBUMBASHI. Made in Lubumbashi.

I thanked and hugged her.

Then she pointed out that one of the stones was missing. Number 24. She had no idea how, when or where it had gone missing. Nestling in its place on the cotton wool was a shiny little Christmas tree light.

That night, before I fell into sleep, I thought about the missing stone, wondering what had happened to it.

Then a gentle thought passed whimsically through my mind.

Perhaps the missing stone was the pink crystal my friend Steven had given me to bury in the DRC.

For peace in Africa.